INDIAN CIVILIZATION AND THE SCIENCE OF FINGERPRINTING

INDIAN CIVILIZATION AND THE SCIENCE OF FINGERPRINTING

Dr. G. S. Sodhi and Dr. Jasjeet Kaur

PUBLICATIONS DIVISION
Ministry of Information and Broadcasting
Government of India

2013 (Saka 1935)

PD BN ISBN : 978-81-230-1811-9
S&T-ENG-OP-12-2013-14

Price : ₹160.00

Published by Additional Director General, Publications Division, Ministry of Information and Broadcasting, Government of India, Soochna Bhawan, C.G.O. Complex, Lodhi Road, New Delhi - 110003

http://www.publicationsdivision.nic.in

Editor : Nitima Shiv Charan
Cover Design : Gajanan P. Dhope

Sales Centres: • Soochna Bhawan, CGO Complex, Lodhi Road, **New Delhi-**110003 • Hall No. 196, Old Secretariat, **Delhi-**110054 • 701, B Wing, 7th Floor, Kendriya Sadan, Belapur, **Navi Mumbai-**400614 • 8, Esplanade East, **Kolkata-**700069 • 'A' Wing, Rajaji Bhawan, Besant Nagar, **Chennai-**600090 • Bihar Satate Co-operative Bank Building, Ahoka Rajpath, **Patna-**80004 • Press Road, Near Govt. Press, **Thiruvanthapuram-**695001. • Hall No. 1, 2nd Floor, Kendriya Bhawan, Sector H, Aliganj, **Lucknow-**226024 • Hall No. Gruhakalpa Complex, M.G. Road, Namplally, **Hyderabad-**500001 • 1st Floor, 'F' Wing, Kendriya Sadan, Koramangala, **Bengaluru-**560034 • Ambica Complex, 1st Floor, Paldi, **Ahmedabad-**380007 • House No. 07, New Colony, Chenikurthi, K.K.B. Road, **Guwahati-**781003

Typesetting : S S Graphix, G. P. Main Road, Kalkaji, New Delhi - 110 019

Printed by : Salasar Imaging Systems, New Delhi-110 035

Preface

It may be asserted that there is no more effective deterrent to crime than the certainty of detection. Equally true is that there is no surer way to establishing identity than by fingerprints. The detection of fingerprints at the scene of crime is therefore one of the most powerful tools available in casework investigations.

The science of fingerprinting originated in India. Indians were not only aware of the importance of this discipline, but were also quite passionate to take it to great heights. It was this passion which brought about the metamorphosis of fingerprinting from a mere curiosity stage to a more sophisticated stage where it replaced all other trivial systems of identification.

In the last decade of nineteenth century, two Indian officers of the Bengal Police, Sub-Inspectors Azizul Haque and Hem Chandra Bose worked out a mathematical formula for classifying fingerprints. This formula was soon adopted by all the nations across the globe for cataloguing criminal record. Unfortunately, due to the imperialist policies of the colonial rulers, the Indian policemen were sidelined and their English officer, Sir Edward Richard Henry shrewdly gave his name to the classification methodology.

This text has been written with two aims: Firstly, to highlight that the science of fingerprinting has always been a part of Indian culture and civilization and secondly, to give due credit to the Indian police officers who, despite their pioneering and innovative work on fingerprints, never got the recognition they deserved.

Prior to 1950s, the locution *fingerprint* was scripted as *finger print* or *finger-print*. While quoting the historical documents and archive records, we have retained the original textual style.

Dr. G. S. Sodhi
Dr. Jasjeet Kaur

Acknowledgements

We wish to thank –

Indian National Science Academy, New Delhi for sanctioning a research project on history of fingerprinting.

National Archives of India, New Delhi for granting permission to survey Home Department Records.

National Crime Records Bureau, New Delhi for information on fingerprint cataloguing system.

Bureau of Police Research and Development, New Delhi for access to reference material on fingerprints.

Indian Council of Historical Research, New Delhi for literature on Mughal edicts.

Maharaja Ranjit Singh Museum, Amritsar for a photograph of the hand print of Maharaja Ranjit Singh.

Bhuri Singh Museum, Chamba for photographs of hand prints of Raja Brajraj Dev and Shah Zaman.

The Fingerprint Society, U.K. for instituting annual awards in the names of Azizul Haque and Hem Chandra Bose in recognition to their contributions in the area of fingerprints.

International Police Organisation, Lyon, France for sending a note by Ministry of Interior, Germany on the contribution of Hem Chandra Bose to single digit fingerprint classification system.

H.E. Tariq A. Karim, Hon'ble High Commissioner for Bangladesh to India for reading material and references on Azizul Haque.

Mohiuddin Ahmed for relating incidents from the personal life of Azizul Haque.

Fehmina Rehman for highlighting the contributions of Azizul Haque and Hem Chandra Bose to fingerprinting through internet.

John Berry, Hertfordshire, U.K., former editor, *Fingerprint Whorld* for providing biography of Sir Edward Richard Henry and a copy of Belper Commission Report on Fingerprints.

Sartaj Singh, Director, Fingerprint Bureau, Punjab Police Academy, Phillaur for information on the types and patterns of fingerprints.

Contents

Introduction

WHETHER ONE BELIEVES in the theological origin of man or goes with the anthropological school of thought, there can be no doubt that each person is individualized by his or her fingerprints. Today, fingerprint individuality is accepted and taken for granted all over the world, but only when we go back into the history of this discipline do we realize that Indians knew about the relevance and significance of fingerprinting before any other civilization had an inkling of it. Since the dawn of recorded history, till the present times, Indians have consistently studied and researched this branch of knowledge, traversing from initial speculation, through interpretation, to its development into the most perfect system of identification.

In the ancient era, Indians contemplated the designs on fingers and hands from an astrological point of view.

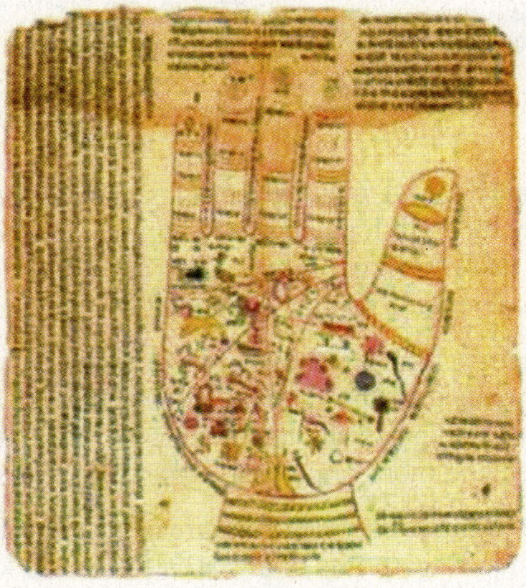

In ancient era fingerprints and palm prints were studied to make astrological predictions

In the medieval era they became cognizant of the fact that the hand print of each person is unique. Several edicts and documents of this period bear the hand print of the author instead of or in addition to his seal/signatures. as one below.

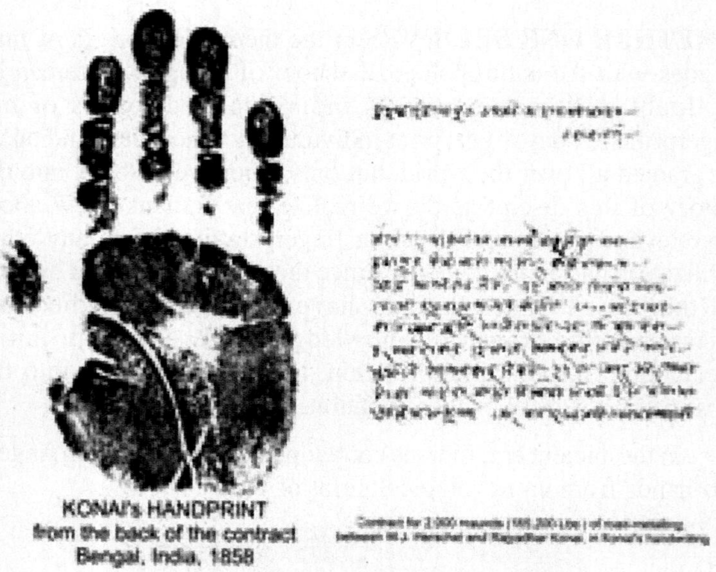

Hand print on a document

At the interface of medieval era and modern era, Indians realized, partly by erudition and partly by ingeniousness, that the impression of just one finger is enough to establish identity. Thus thumb print evolved as a simpler substitute of hand print.

The modern period saw the establishment of the world's first fingerprint bureau in India. It was named *Bengal Fingerprint Bureau* and was set up at Calcutta in 1897. With that, the study of fingerprints became more organized, systematic and scientific.

It was at Bengal Fingerprint Bureau that the formula for classifying all ten fingerprints of a person for record keeping was worked out. More than one hundred years later this method is still being followed in all the civilized nations of the world.

Later, a single fingerprint classification system, as well as a telegraphic code for transmitting fingerprints from one crime record office to another was also developed at the Bengal Fingerprint Bureau. The techniques for detecting fingerprints at crime scenes, the procedures for recording the fingerprints of arrested suspects and the scheme for comparing the detected and recorded fingerprints too were standardized here.

Fingerprints now superseded all previous methods of establishing identities of criminals.

With passage of time, these also evolved as a means to prevent crime.

Still later, fingerprints began to be used for personal identification for humanitarian reasons, such as in cases of amnesia, missing persons or unknown deceased. In addition, they proved invaluable in identifying victims of arson, floods and air crashes.

Basis of Fingerprint Identification

FINGERPRINTS ARE the distinctive ridges that appear as corrugated lines on the bulbs of fingers and thumbs. The corrugation results due to rising of a portion of the upper layer of fingertip skin slightly above the normal level. Since the upper layer of skin is called *epidermis*, the finger ridges are also referred to as *epidermal ridges*. The depression between two ridges is called a *furrow*. The ridges and furrows form a complex, curved pattern on the fingertips.

Ridges and furrows form a complex, curved pattern on fingertips

The pattern on each finger of a person is so unique that it is not repeated on another finger of the same person or on the fingers of any other person. This makes fingerprints the most infallible means of identification.

Functions of finger ridges

Epidermal ridges have an average width of 0.48 millimeters in males and 0.43 millimeters in females. These perform the following two functions.

1. *They increase security of contact with objects*. The ridges are studded with small holes, called sweat pores through which perspiration is exuded. The perspiration acts as a lubricant and ensures firmness of grip.

2. *They enhance the sense of touch*. When a finger comes into contact with an uneven surface, the epidermal ridges amplify the vibrations caused due to friction and transmit the signal to sensory nerves involved in texture perception, increasing the sense of touch. For this reason, epidermal ridges are also called *friction ridges*.

Fundamental principles of fingerprinting

The science of identification by screening and comparing fingerprints is called *dactyloscopy*. This science is based on the following three principles.

1. *No two persons and no two fingers of the same person have identical ridge design on the fingertips*. Fingerprints are absolutely unique – more unique than the DNA, the genetic material in the human cells. Although identical twins have the same DNA sequence, they do not have identical fingerprints.

2. *The fingerprints remain unchanged throughout life*. The ridge pattern begins to take shape during fetal stage and does not alter during a person's lifespan. It is only after death that decomposition sets in and the finger ridges are destroyed. Figures (A) and (B) are the fingerprints of a child, recorded at the age of 2 and 15 years respectively. The prints do not show any variation.

(A) (B)

Fingerprints of a child recorded with a time lag of about 13 years show no variations

In the growing age, the fingerprint patterns expand; as a result of aging, these may shrink. However, the basic design remains unaffected – and unique.

3. *Fingerprints can be classified for record keeping*. When a person commits a crime and is arrested, he is fingerprinted by the police. The fingerprint record is then passed on to the nearest fingerprint bureau. There are about twenty five state-level fingerprint bureaus in India. Their functioning is coordinated by *Central Fingerprint Bureau, Ministry of Home Affairs*. Each bureau maintains a fingerprint record of a few lakh criminals – and the records are piling up.

Just as the books are catalogued in a library, there is a procedure for classifying the fingerprint record too.

Fingerprint record of criminals can be catalogued

The method of classifying criminal record was worked out in India – and by Indians – and is being followed around the globe. It is so fool-proof that it takes just a few minutes to locate the fingerprint slip of a particular suspect out of a few lakh slips. We will discuss the details of the classification procedure in a later chapter (p.46).

Fingerprinting is a component of the larger discipline of biometry. The latter uses a person's physical parameters, such as the network of retina nerves, pitch of voice and facial characters for identifying him. However, fingerprinting is the only constituent of biometry which can be catalogued for record.

Fingerprint patterns

The finger ridges have definite contours and appear in three broad patterns: Arches, loops and whorls. These are presented in the figure below.

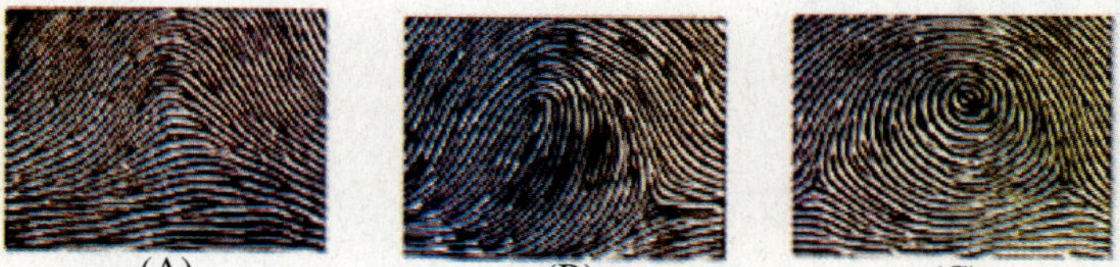

(A) (B) (C)

Three patterns of fingerprints. (A) arches; (B) loops; and (C) whorls

In *arches*, the ridges enter on one side of the finger impression, rise and then flow out on the other side, giving the shape of a tent. In *loops*, the ridges enter on either side of the imprint, re-curve, and terminate on the same side. The loops which flow towards the little finger are called *ulnar* loops, while those which flow in the direction of the thumb are called *radial* loops. In *whorls* the ridges form a circular pattern.

The ridges in each pattern seem to be running parallel to each other. However, closer inspection reveals that the parallel ridge flow is interrupted by the following seven types of irregularities, which are collectively referred to as *fingerprint characters* or *ridge characters* or *minutiae*.

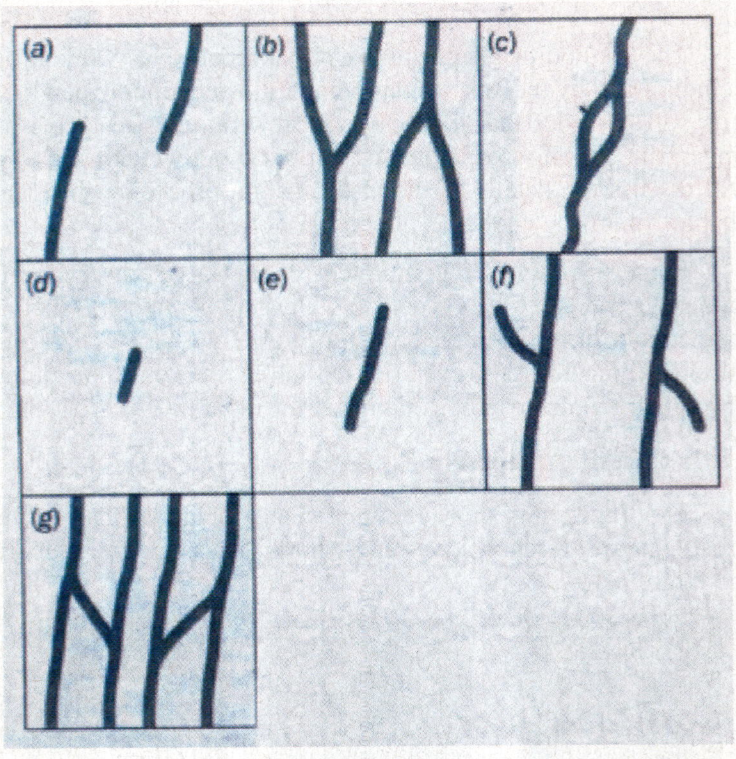

Fingerprint characters

(a) *Ridge termination* – when the ridge flow abruptly ends.

(b) *Bifurcation* – when the ridge splits into two, making a 'Y'.

(c) *Lake* – when there is an enclosed area in between the ridge.

(d) *Island* – when there is a small dot or circle within the overall pattern.

(e) *Short independent ridge* – when there is a relatively small ridge within the overall pattern.

(f) *Hook or spur* – when a small curved ridge is attached to a regular ridge.

(g) *Crossover* – when two parallel ridges are joined by a small ridge.

For example, in the fingerprint pattern depicted in the following figure, three minutiae are marked.

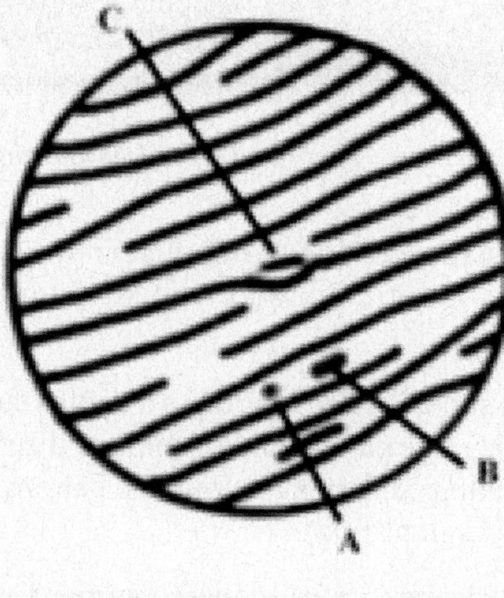

Minutiae within the overall ridge pattern

Minutia A is an island; B is a short independent ridge; and C is a lake.

It is the combination of the minutiae that makes each fingerprint unique. In no two fingers identical minutiae would occupy exactly similar positions, even if the overall ridge pattern (arch, loop or whorl) is the same. In case of identical twins, the overall ridge pattern on similar fingers of the siblings is identical. For example, if one sibling has whorl pattern on the index finger of right hand, the other sibling too will have whorl pattern on the right index finger.

The overall pattern on similar fingers of identical twins in same

Nevertheless, the location of minutiae in the two fingers will vary. Thus even identical twins can be individualized by fingerprints.

If a finger is superficially injured to a depth of one millimeter or less, a part of the ridge pattern and/or some of the ridge characters get temporarily damaged. Upon healing, the pattern and characters reappear in their original form.

However, a deeper injury causes permanent damage to a portion of ridge pattern and ridge characters. In such cases a scar remains even after the finger is healed Yet it does not render the fingerprint useless as far as identification is concerned.

A scar in the fingerprint

On an average, there are about 80 ridge characters in a fingerprint. Even if one-tenth of these can be visualized, the identity of a person can be established.

Fingerprinting in Ancient India

SINCE ANCIENT TIMES, fingerprinting has remained intertwined with the Indian culture. An Indian scripture, *Samudra Shastra,* compiled by a sage named Samudra Rishi in 3102 BC, tells us a great deal about fingerprinting. As stated in the previous chapter, fingerprint patterns may be classified into three broad types: Arches, loops and whorls (p.7). The present day fingerprint examiners have noted that statistically, 5% of fingerprints have arch pattern, 60% are loops and 35% are whorls. *Samudra Shastra* too identifies three types of fingerprints. It says that two are of common types, viz., *sankha* (corresponding to loops), and *chakra* (corresponding to whorls), while the third type, *seep* (corresponding to arches) are rare. It is not surprising that the fingerprint examiners of modern era and Samudra Rishi of ancient era reached the same conclusion. The astonishing fact is that what the experts inferred merely one hundred years ago, the holy man could ratiocinate more than 5000 years ago! There is no written record on description of fingerprints prior to *Samudra Shastra.*

The modern science of fingerprinting asserts that parallel ridges on fingertips are interrupted by seven types of irregularities, known as *fingerprint characters* or *minutiae.* These are described on p.8. *Samudra Shastra* too identifies many of these characters.

For example, *apuran java, puran java, padam* and *aax* are concurrent to *bifurcation, lake, hook* and *island* respectively, of modern fingerprint discipline. *Nirpaax* and *kundla* are close to island, while *kamal* is close to lake. *Toran* appears similar to crossover.

The fact that the portrayal of fingerprint characters in *Samudra Shastra* is far less tangible than what it is now reflects the limitations of technology when the scripture was written. It is relatively easy to discern the outer pattern of a fingerprint with

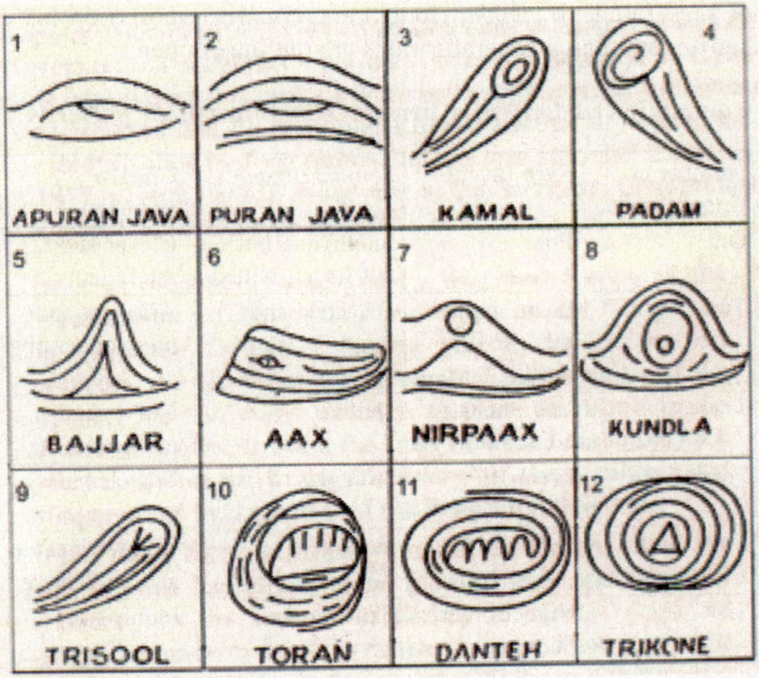

Fingerprint characters as depicted in Samudra Shastra

naked eye, but for locating the minutiae, one has to use a magnifying glass. The first lens was invented around 1 AD. How could *Samudra Rishi* and his disciples decipher the ridge characters, some with perfection and others with blemish, without the aid of a magnifier, is still a mystery.

Nevertheless, it is obvious that the author of *Samudra Shastra* would not have studied such minor details directly from the fingers. This means that he must have developed a method to record the finger impressions on a suitable surface. This also means that he would have designed a version of modern day stamp pad.

It must be acknowledged that *Samudra Shastra* does not correlate the ridge patterns or ridge characters with identification. It deals with astrology – the science of predicting the future. It advocates that the destiny of a person is controlled by the number of *seep* (arches), *sankha* (loops) and *chakra* (whorls) on his or her fingers. Some generalizations are outlined in here.

Correlation of trait of a person with fingerprint patterns

Number of fingers with	***Seep* (arches)**	***Sankha* (loops)**	***Chakra* (whorls)**
One	Poor	Intelligent, but not strong-willed	Clever and intelligent
Two	Lazy; wastes inherited wealth	Detached and saintly	Arrogant and non-cooperative
Three	Yogi; health conscious	Dull	Not a good person
Four	Living in poverty	Struggles to rise	Traveler
Five	Lucky	Intelligent	Knowledgeable and inquisitive
Six	Higher order thinking	Extravagant	Inquisitive
Seven	Successful	Poor	Interested in poetry and music
Eight	Struggles to achieve in life	Leading a happy life	Wealthy and courageous
Nine	Infamous	Wealthy through fraud	Knowledgeable and interested in yoga
Ten	Popular and respected	Aristocrat, but humble	Very lucky and popular

All astrologers do not agree with these generalizations. *Samudra Shastra* itself says that the number of patterns on fingertips is not the only parameter for prediction of a person's traits. True forecast can be made only if the fingerprint patterns are mediated in concert with the types of designs in other parts of the palm.

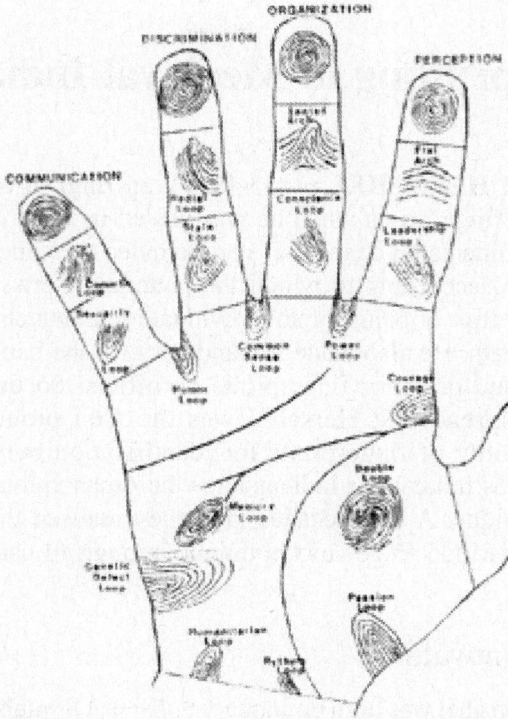

For astrological predictions, the fingerprint patterns should be studied in combination with patterns on palm

However, such details are beyond the scope of the present text. It suffices to say that since in the ancient era the Indians studied the ridge patterns of the fingers and the palms so minutely, and so meticulously, by the beginning of the medieval era they could perceive the utility of hand prints for identification purposes.

Fingerprinting in Medieval India

SIR WILLIAM HERSCHEL (1833-1917), an English officer, started studying fingerprints when he was posted in India during the later half of nineteenth century. He propounded the concept of ridge persistency, according to which the patterns of criss-cross lines on the fingertips or palms of an individual remain unchanged from birth till death. He also made it mandatory for the natives to impress their hand prints or fingerprints on official documents. Word quickly spread that Herschel was the first pioneer to recognize the utility of fingerprints for identification purposes. However, this was fallacy, for Indians knew beforehand that each palm print is unique. A few decades later they realised that the impression of just one finger too is unique enough to establish identity.

Herschel's Innovation

William Herschel was born on January 9, 1833 at Slough, U.K. His interest in overseas trading prompted him to join the Haileybury College. This institution imparted training in administration to those aspiring to work with the East India Company. In 1853, when Herschel was 20 years old, the Company deputed him to Bengal. After the First War of Independence (1857), the Company was taken over by the British Crown and Herschel automatically became a member of the Indian Civil Service. He was posted at Jungipoor.

It was here that Herschel, on behalf of the government, entered in an agreement with a local contractor, Rajyadhar Konai, for supplying material for the construction of roads. In order to authenticate the covenant, Herschel asked Konai to place his right hand print on the agreement. Konai obliged by the conditions of the contract.

Sir William Herschel

Subsequently, Herschel realized that it was more advantageous to use the impressions of right index and middle fingers as against using the whole hand.

In 1877 Herschel was appointed the Magistrate and Collector of Hooghly. The courts, the prison, the deed registration office and the pension office now fell under his purview. He, therefore, decided to put the fingerprint system to practical usage. He introduced the practice of taking pensioners' fingerprints to avoid impersonation by others after their (pensioners') death. He also made it mandatory on the part of the concerned individuals to put their finger impressions on the legal deeds.

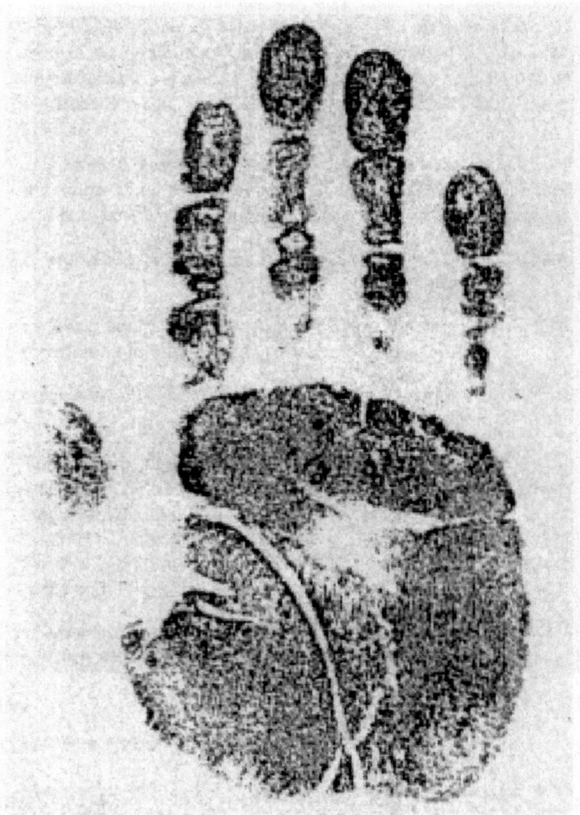

Hand print of Rajyadhar Konai (1858)

In 1916, Herschel published a book entitled, *The Origin of Finger-Printing*, in which he took pains to emphasize that Konai's contract was the first official document bearing the hand print as a mark of personal identification. In the preface, Herschel writes:

> The following pages have two objectives: first, to place on record the genesis of the finger-print method of personal identification; secondly, to examine the scanty suggestions of evidence that this use of our fingers had been foreshadowed in Europe…

> ....I believe these pages will suffice to show the originality of my study of its two essential features, the strict individuality and the stubborn persistence of the patterns on our fingers.

Why did Herschel ask Konai to put his hand impression on the contract? In his own words:

> ....I was only wishing to frighten Konai out of all thought of repudiating his signature hereafter.

Almost a hundred years later, an important website on history of fingerprinting (*www.onin.com/fp/fphistory*.html) corroborates Herschel's point of view:

> The English first began using fingerprints in July of 1858, when Sir William Herschel had Rajyadhar Konai, a local businessman, impress his hand print on the back of a contract.... The native was suitably impressed, and Herschel made a habit of requiring palm prints....on every contract made with the locals.

Rajyadhar Konai fulfilled the conditions of the agreement not because he was afraid, but because he, being an Indian, understood the significance of hand prints.

A Customary Practice

Herschel further writes in his book:

> Many must have heard of some such use of a man's hand; and the correspondence that has taken place has brought to light old instances of the hand, or the nail of a finger, or the teeth in one's mouth, being used to certify a man's act or a women's. But these have all been isolated instances.

These were not isolated instances. It was rather a common practice among rulers of medieval India to sign the routine documents, but to put their hand prints on more important ones. The following figure shows the hand impression of Mughal Emperor Shah Jahan. This has been reproduced from a *farman* (royal edict) addressed by the Emperor to Dalan Singh, the king of Gidhour (in present day Bihar).

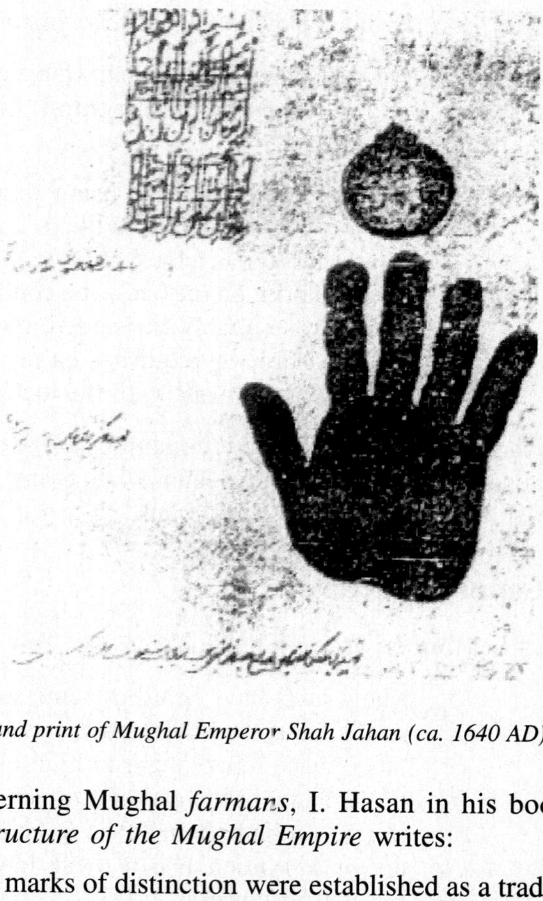

Hand print of Mughal Emperor Shah Jahan (ca. 1640 AD)

Concerning Mughal *farmans*, I. Hasan in his book, *The Central Structure of the Mughal Empire* writes:

Three marks of distinction were established as a tradition by which the king, according to the rank of the addressee and the extent of favor desired to be bestowed upon him, could exalt him.

1. By putting his signature in addition to the official seal.

2. By adding a line or two at the top in his own hand…

3. By putting the mark of the royal hand on the *farman*.

The following two examples support Hasan's assertion.

(a) In 1636 AD (1046 AH), the joint forces of Shah Jahan and 'Adil Khan, under the command of Khan Zaman Bahadur, invaded the camp of Shahuji Bhosle, the ruler of Poona (in present day Maharashtra). The joint army defeated Shahuji, who was compelled to accept the terms of peace. *Badshah Nama*, the biography of Shah Jahan relates:

> Since the garrison (of Shahuji) was now reduced to great extremities ….Shahuji wrote frequently to Khan Bahadur in the most humble strain, promising to pay allegiance to the crown. He at the same time solicited a written treaty …stamped with the impression of his hand.

(b) In 1613 AD (1022 AH), Mughal Emperor Jahangir defeated Amar Singh Sisodia, the ruler of Udaipur (in present day Rajasthan). The following is recorded in *Tuzuk-i-Jahangiri*, the biography of Jahangir:

> When Rana Amar Singh Sisodiya of Udaipur was brought under the yoke of obedience, he demanded the royal *panja* as a condition of treaty….and the condition was complied with.

Rulers other than those belonging to the Mughal dynasty were also aware of the importance of hand prints/fingerprints.The figure shown below depicts the hand print of Maharaja Ranjit Singh. This has been reproduced from a treaty dated April 13, 1827 AD between the Maharaja and Fateh Singh, the king of Kapurthala (in present day Punjab).

Hand print of Maharaja Ranjit Singh on a treaty (1827 AD)

A royal edict bearing the hand print of Raja Brajraj Dev of Jammu is reprinted herein. This followed the conquest of Basohli

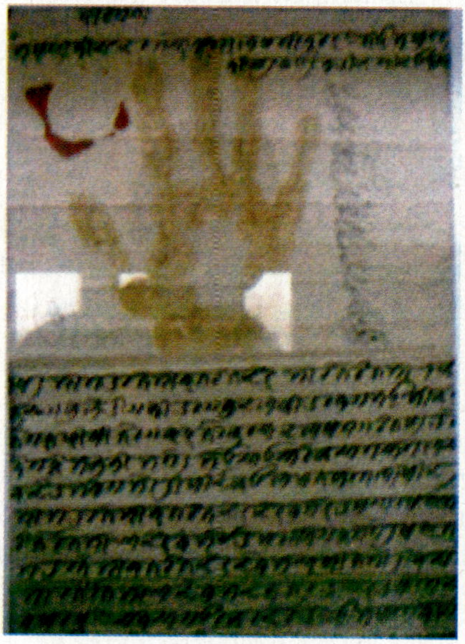

Hand print of Raja Brajraj Dev (1783 AD)

by Raja Raj Singh of Chamba in 1782 AD. Dated 18th of *Bhadon* of Sastra year 59 AD (1783), the edict restores the parganas of Jundh, Bhalai, Diur, Bhundal and Kihar to the kingdom of Chamba.

The following figure depicts the hand print of Shah Zaman, the ruler of Deccan who, in 1794, occupied Lahore. In the hand print-bearing edict, scripted in Persian, Shah Zaman authorises Raja Jit Singh of Chamba to discharge some of the official duties of the Deccan state in his absence.

Hand print of Shah Zaman (1794 AD)

Herschel's Delusion

We are not sure whether Herschel was aware of the hand-printed documents of medieval India. Perhaps he was not. Nevertheless, he asserts that the true essence of hand prints/fingerprints lies in identification. He further states that neither the custom of *tep-sai* – the practice followed by illiterates in Bengal to wet the tip of finger by ink and press it on a document – nor the convention followed by Chinese bankers to put their thumb impressions on currency notes had anything to do with identification.

Herschel thus believed that by recording Konai's hand print, he was the first to hit upon the idea of identification by fingerprints. So sure was Herschel about his innovation that in October 1917, he sent the following note to the Secretary, Government of Bengal for favor of placement in the archives records:

> I have the honour to send you by this mail a copy of the pamphlet which I have lately published on the 'Origin of Finger-printing', which I request you to lay before His Excellency the Governor for favourable consideration of the purpose I have in view: which is to place on record in the archives of his Government the story of what I may now with perfect confidence call 'the Discovery' of the peculiar value of finger prints by a member of the Bengal Civil Service.
>
> I recall these facts as necessary to fill up the record of my share in what has grown to be a world-wide and powerful instrument for the security of society in various ways, all tending, I venture to think, to realize the hope I had expressed in 1877 that 'its general use would be a substantial contribution towards public morality'. Looking back now, forty years after my retirement, I wish that I had rather said 'towards confidence between man and man'.

Herschel advocates in his book that most authors have failed to realize the force of the word 'identification' in the fingerprint system:

> It (identification) means that if a man can be indicated whose fingerprint agrees with that on a document, he is identified with the man who put that one there. That is all we want. But it will be seen that there must be two impressions

> at least, that will bear comparison, to constitute 'identification'.

Most of the hand-printed documents of medieval India represented a formally concluded and ratified proclamation between the rulers. As is customary, a copy of such an agreement would have been kept by all those who were party to it. This very well satisfies the criterion which, according to Herschel, is necessary for identification.

We once again refer to the hand print-bearing treaty which Shahuji Bhosle solicited from Shah Jahan. Normally the victorious ruler dictates the conditions of the treaty. But here is a case where a king, who is at a receiving end, lays down the terms for peace. By asking for a hand-printed document, Bhosle was trying to ensure that the covenant be respected by the descendents of the warring factions. What was special about the hand print, save it being a mode of identification?

Moreover, regarding Mughal *farmans*, I. Hasan in his book, *The Central Structure of the Mughal Empire* writes:

> The procedure in drafting the *farmans* was very elaborate. Having regard to the conditions of the age in which the Mughals ruled, every necessary precaution was taken to safeguard against frauds in this connection.

The fact that hand print was duly safeguarded clearly indicates its utility as a means of identification.

Herschel concludes his book, *The Origin of Finger-Printing* by stating:

> ....It is hard to believe that a system so practically useful as this could have been known in the great lands of the East for generations past, without arresting the notice of Western statesmen, merchants, travelers and students. Yet the knowledge never reached us.

Many foreign visitors to India did notice the practice of hand-printing, but took it as a superstitious custom of the natives.

However, Hasan states:

> The mark of the royal hand was the highest distinction (on a *farman)*...
>
> I have not found any case in which it (hand print) was put on a *farman* to any royal servant...

Thus the hand impression signatures were put only on those official documents that were sent to individuals of status. These were generally rulers of other provinces so that they may recognize the sovereignty (read individuality) of the sender. Hence such deeds were outside the purview of commoners.

Nevertheless, there were some enterprising westerners who unearthed such documents for academic exercises. However, these investigators were neither civil servants nor scientists, but mainly historians. One such historian was E.B. Havell from whose text, *A Handbook to Agra and the Taj*, we have reprinted the hand impression of Shah Jahan (p.20). Havell was an Englishman who came to India to research the Mughal history, but finally settled in this country. W.E. Begley who, along with Z.A. Desai, translated Shah Jahan's biography, *Badshah Nama*, from Persian to English, is an American historian. He too has referred to the hand-printed documents of the Mughal era. Going by their professional training, however, such researchers were interested in the contents of treaties and not in the symbols of identification.

Indian Contribution in Modern Era

IN 1897, the world's first fingerprint bureau was set up in Calcutta (now Kolkata). Christened, *Bengal Fingerprint Bureau*, it was housed in the Writers' Building.

Writers' Building during British times

At that time, a very large section of Indian population was illiterate. Instead of appending their signatures on official documents, most persons used to impress their hand prints. With passage of time, hand print gave way to impressions of index and ring fingers.

About two years before the inauguration of the Bengal Fingerprint Bureau, the deed registration office proposed a landmark amendment regarding fingerprint signatures. Khan Bahadur Delawar Hosain Ahmed, Inspector General of Registration in a note (no. 4655, dated October 12, 1895) addressed to the Chief Secretary, Government of Bengal stated:

> Originally the impression of the registrant's first and third fingers were taken, but….the thumb mark alone is most suitable for ….ready identification because (a) its impression is much larger than that of the fingers, and the pattern can be read easily without magnifying power, and (b) the question would never arise as to which digit was actually used in making the impression if the thumb was used.

By the time the Bengal Fingerprint Bureau was inaugurated, the thumb impression became an acceptable form of signature not only on registration deeds, but on all official documents including bank accounts, pension records and postal transactions. The impression of any other finger too served the purpose, but the thumb impression was preferred (and is still preferred) as it has a larger pattern area as compared to other digits.

For cataloguing criminal record, however, the impressions of all ten fingers were required.

Therefore, whenever a suspect was arrested the impressions of all his ten fingers were taken and preserved for record keeping. A method of classifying fingerprint record was invented at the Bengal Fingerprint Bureau. Later a single digit classification system, which required the impression of just one finger for cataloguing of criminal record, was also worked out. A method of telegraphically communicating the single fingerprint from one bureau to another too was innovated here.

For day to day working, the Bengal Fingerprint Bureau standardized the procedures for lifting fingerprints at crime scenes, for recording fingerprints of arrested suspects and for comparing two or more fingerprints to establish the correct identity. It also prepared protocols for different types of fingerprints that are encountered while solving crime cases.

Types of fingerprints

Fingerprints are categorized into the following four types.

1. **Inked prints**. Also called *exemplar prints* or *known prints*, inked fingerprints are those which are deliberately collected from a subject for –
   - Comparison with fingerprints found at the scene of crime.
   - Maintaining record of habitual criminals.
   - Impeaching a defendant by proof of prior conviction.
   - Enrollment of law abiding citizens within a system, for example, on application forms for seeking academic admissions, employment, passports, visas or financial transactions.

Inked fingerprints may be used for enrollment within a system

2. **Latent prints.** The term latent means hidden. Accordingly, latent fingerprints are those which are invisible. These are accidently left by a suspect at the crime scene. For this reason these are also referred to as *chance fingerprints*.

   Latent fingerprints are formed by sweat. When a suspect touches an object at the crime scene, he leaves a deposition of perspiration secreted by sweat glands embedded beneath the ridges of his fingers. This deposition forms exactly the same pattern on the object as is the ridge design on the fingertip. The sweat glands beneath the fingertips are called *eccrine glands* and their secretion is called *eccrine sweat.*

   There are chances that before touching an object, the suspect may have swabbed his fingers on his face, neck or hair. The sweat glands associated with these body parts are called *sebaceous glands*. Their secretion, called *sebaceous sweat*, supplements the eccrine sweat deposition.

   Thus a latent fingerprint is generally formed by a mixture of eccrine sweat and sebaceous sweat. Being colorless, the sweat deposition is not visible to the naked eye. It may, however, be visualized by chemical treatment.

3. **Patent prints.** Like latent fingerprints, patent imprints too are chance impressions. They are left accidently at a crime scene. However, unlike latent prints, these are not invisible. They are formed by the transfer of foreign material from a finger on to a surface. If the fingers of a suspect are coated with clay, dust, flour, ink or blood and they touch a clean, smooth object, then patent prints appear due to the deposition of these contaminants on the item. For example, the patent prints shown below were formed when blood-coated fingers of a person were pressed against a wall.

   Patent fingerprints are not developed by chemical treatment but are directly photographed.

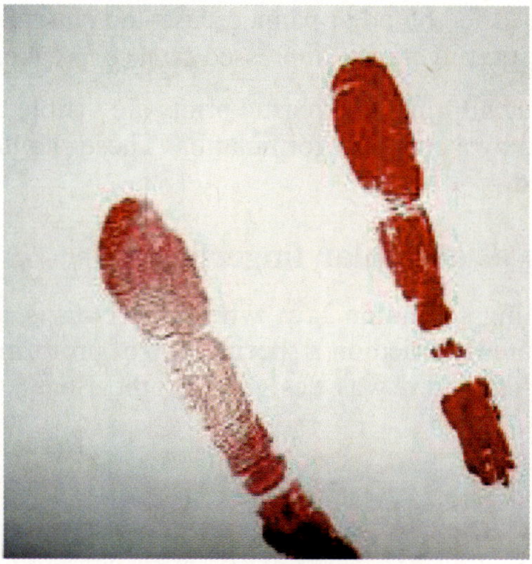

Patent prints made by blood soaked fingers on a wall

4. **Plastic prints.** If the fingers of a suspect are clean, and are impressed on a soft material that retains the ridge details, the resulting impressions are called plastic prints. Common materials on which plastic prints may be found are wax, clay,

A plastic fingerprint on a soap cake

partially dried blood or paint, grease and putty. Shown below is a plastic fingerprint impressed on a soap cake.

Like patent prints, the plastic prints are visible and need not be developed by a chemical formulation. These should be directly photographed.

Recording of exemplar fingerprints

According to Indian law, when a person is arrested, his fingerprints are recorded on a special type of proforma, called the *index card*. This card was designed by the Bengal Fingerprint

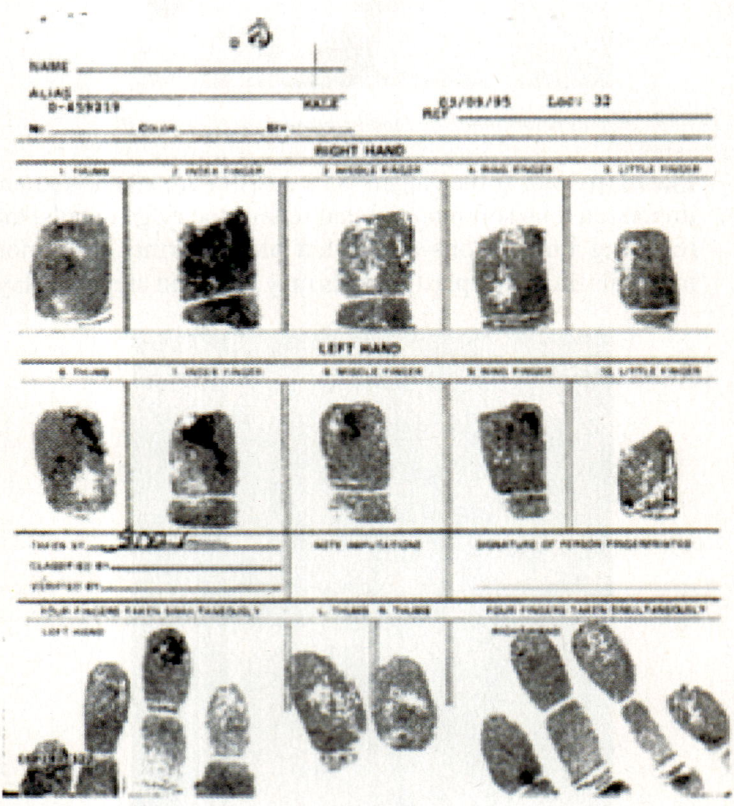

An index card

Bureau and later modified by the *Central Fingerprint Bureau*, under the aegis of *National Crime Records Bureau, Ministry of Home Affairs*. An index card is displayed in the following figure.

The index card has three sections, one each for recording the–

(a) Personal details of the subject.

(b) Rolled fingerprint impressions.

(c) Plain fingerprint impressions.

The first section has columns to enter the name, gender, address, aliases of the suspect, as well as the police station under the jurisdiction of which the crime was committed. These details are filled up before taking the finger impressions.

The subject is then asked to wash his hands so as to remove dirt and perspiration. The hands are then dried with a towel, but care should be taken that no lint adheres to the subject's fingers. For recording the finger impressions – both the rolled and the plain ones – the index card is placed on a table, the height of which can

A table used for recording exemplar fingerprints

be adjusted with regard to the height of the suspect. The latter is made to stand erect before the table and the movements of his fingers, while recording the fingerprints, are controlled by an experienced fingerprint expert.

The second section of the index card has ten boxes arranged in two rows of five each. The upper row is for recording the rolled impressions of four fingers and thumb of right hand of the suspect, while the lower row is for the corresponding digits of his left hand. The order in each row, from left to right is: Thumb, index finger, middle finger, ring finger and little finger.

Each finger is rolled on a fingerprint ink pad from nail edge to nail edge, so that an even, thin layer of ink gets applied on the finger, from just below the tip to about a quarter inch below the first joint.

A fingerprint ink pad

An inked finger

The inked finger is then rolled, nail edge to nail edge, in the relevant box on the index card. Whether on the fingerprint pad or on the index card, the fingers are rolled away from the subject's body, while the thumbs are rolled towards the subject's body.

Recording rolled fingerprints

The rolled impressions cover the total surface area of the fingertips, and provide the entire ridge pattern needed for classification of fingerprints, as well as necessary number of ridge characters needed for proper identification. Since these impressions are recorded successively for each finger, there are chances that a clever suspect may impress the print of a particular finger in the box meant for a different finger. This would lead to incorrect classification.

To avoid this problem, the third and last section of the index card has space for plain impressions, also called *flat prints* or *slap prints*. On the left side of the index card, the impressions of all the fingers of left hand, starting from little finger and ending at thumb are recorded, while on the right side, the digits of right hand, from thumb to little finger are imprinted. The fingerprint expert holds the wrist of the subject and impresses all five inked fingers of his left hand in the space meant for plain impressions. He then repeats the operation with the right hand of the suspect. This procedure rules out the scope for manipulation since the impressions of all the fingers of a hand are recorded simultaneously. In fact, the plain impressions are used to verify the sequence and accuracy of rolled prints.

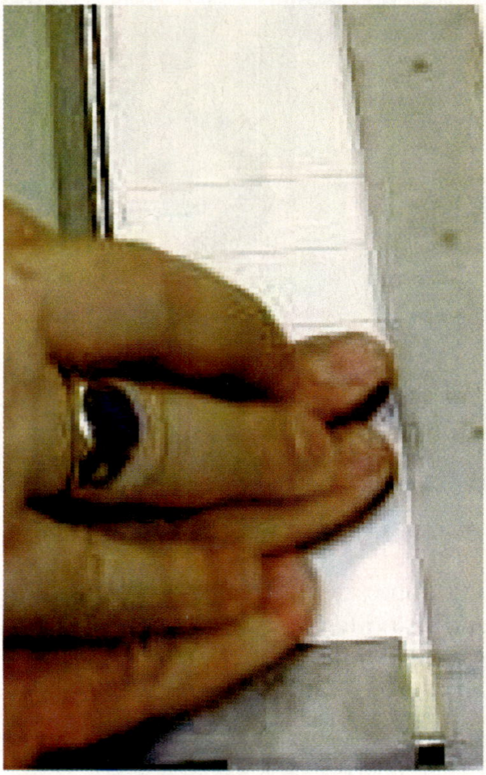

Recording plain impressions

The expert who guides the subject during recording of fingerprints has to be careful on two counts. Firstly, he should not apply too much pressure while impressing the fingers on the index card, otherwise the prints tend to get smudged. Secondly, he should direct the subject to look away from the index card. Experience has shown that prints of better quality are obtained when the subject is relaxed, rather than when he is conscious, while the recording is in process.

Once the index card is ready, the fingerprints are classified and catalogued on the basis of a mathematical formula. This classification formula was worked out in India and – despite the fact that we were under colonial rule – by Indians. We have outlined the classification methodology and described the key role played by Indian police officers in inventing it later in this text.

If the suspect commits another crime and tries to deceive the police by using an alias or by changing his appearance, his index card serves to identify him.

Fingerprints at crime scenes

At a crime scene, an investigator usually comes across latent or hidden fingerprints, although at times, patent and plastic prints may also be encountered. Indian police officers and fingerprint experts are trained to undertake several precautions while searching fingerprints at a site of crime.

Firstly, the investigation officer who visits the crime scene should be fingerprint-conscious. His preliminary order of business should be to cordon off the area where the crime was allegedly committed, so that the fingerprint evidence is not destroyed .

A high-powered torch, endowed with a lens, for locating latent fingerprints

Secondly, the search for fingerprints at a crime site should begin at the entry point itself. By illuminating different zones of the scene by a high-powered torch, the latent prints may be located. The torch should be held at an angle, so that an oblique beam of light falls on different articles.

Thirdly, it should be endeavored to detect, and subsequently develop, as many fingerprints as possible. Latent fingerprints are often weak and faint. After development, their sharpness and clarity is much lower than those of inked prints. Hence many of these do not meet the criteria laid down by the Indian law for fool-proof identification. If a large number of latent prints are lifted from the crime scene, at least a few of these will be sharp enough for correct authentication.

Fourthly, if fingerprints are found on a particular item, the neighboring articles and structures should be carefully examined. For example, while attempting to move a heavy object, the suspect may have pressed his hand on an adjacent wall. As a result, his fingerprints or the entire hand print would be impinged on the wall.

Development of latent fingerprints

Latent fingerprints are formed by deposition of sweat secreted by or adhering to the fingertips on a surface with which the fingers come into contact. Sweat contains 99% water; 0.5% salts, such as those of sodium, potassium, chloride and phosphate; and 0.5% oily components like proteins and fatty acids. All these constituents are colorless and for this reason, latent fingerprints are not visible to the naked eye – hence the term, hidden fingerprints. The sweat deposited by the fingertip on to a surface is called *fingerprint residue*.

The interaction of a chemical formulation with the fingerprint residue converts one or more of the sweat constituents into a colored derivative, so that what is hidden becomes visible and the latent print is said to have developed.

The oldest, simplest and the most common technique of developing latent fingerprints on a hard, smooth surface is the powder method. In the closing years of nineteenth century, Indian fingerprint experts used two types of powders for detection of latent prints: A mercury-based powder and a graphite-based powder. The former, called *hydrargyrum cum creta*, was composed of one part of mercury and two parts of chalk. It was suitable for developing prints on dark colored articles. However, it was withdrawn from use in 1967 when it was realized that mercury posed a health hazard. The graphite powder was effective in developing fingerprints on white colored articles. Even this formulation was withdrawn since graphite particles are extremely light and tend to fly off in outdoor crime scenes.

Commercial fingerprint powders are now available in a variety of shades and hues, although gray and black compositions are most commonly used.

Normally the commercial powders contain a resinous polymer for adhesion (for example, silica, talc, starch) to the sweat deposition and a colorant (for example, charcoal, alizarin) for contrast. These are dusted on the surface containing the latent print and then gently spread with a camel hair brush.

The constituents of the powders interact with water and oily content of fingerprint residue to give a colored impression. Once the color appears, the excess powder is blown off.

When fingerprints are to be developed on a vertical surface, such as a wall or a cupboard, magnetic powders are preferred instead of conventional ones. These contain extremely fine, meshed particles of iron, in addition to the resinous polymer and the colorant.

Magnetic powders are applied with the aid of a special type of brush, called *magnetic brush* or *magna brush* for short. Its bristles are magnetized. The formulation sticks to the magna brush and may be coated on a vertical object or surface.

The developed fingerprints are photographed and then 'lifted' to provide a permanent record. This is done by placing a transparent adhesive tape on the fingerprint area, pressing it and then removing it from the surface.

Lifting of fingerprints for permanent record

The lifted tape, carrying a mirror-image of the developed fingerprints, is pasted on a card which, in turn, is preserved in the record file.

A vapor phase developing technique involves exposing the

An iodine gun

latent fingerprint to iodine fumes. Iodine vapors are directed to the print with the aid of a hand-held equipment called *iodine gun.*

Iodine adheres to the fatty acid constituent of the fingerprint residue, giving brown colored impressions. A limitation of this method is that the developed fingerprints remain visible only for a few minutes and then fade out. Hence these have to be photographed immediately.

Fingerprint developing reagents are available in solution form too. For example, ninhydrin, dissolved in alcohol or petrol, interacts with the protein content of sweat deposition and develops purple colored fingerprints.

Likewise, a solution of silver nitrate in water combines with chloride content of fingerprint residue and develops black colored impressions.

Matching the developed and inked fingerprints

Once a fingerprint has been lifted from a crime scene and subsequently developed, the next stage is to match it with an inked impression procured from the alleged suspect if he has been arrested or from his index card if he had been arrested for a prior conviction.

Comparison of fingerprints is carried out in two steps: Matching the ridge pattern, followed by matching the ridge characters. As stated earlier, the ridge patterns, fall in three broad categories – arches, loops and whorls (p.7). If two fingerprints have different ridge patterns then these definitely belong to different fingers. There is no need to go to the second stage of matching in such cases. For example, the print shown in figure (A) is an arch, while the one depicted in figure (B) is a whorl. The possibility of these belonging to the same finger should be immediately ruled out.

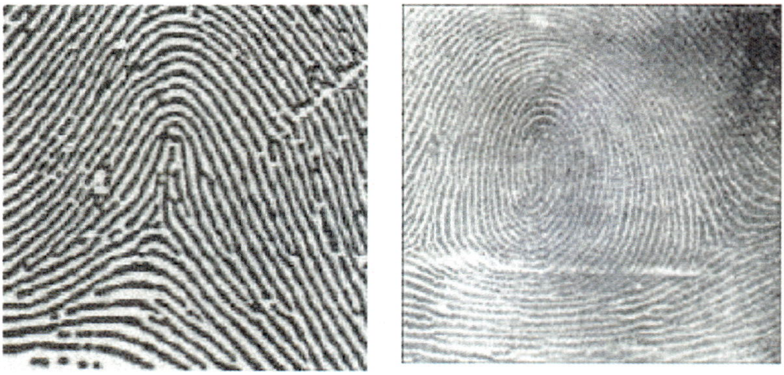

(A) (B)

Prints with different ridge patterns belong to different fingers

If, on the other hand, the patterns are found to be identical, as the ones shown in the figure below – both belong to the whorl category – these may or may not belong to the same finger. In such cases, the comparison moves to the second level – the matching of ridge characters.

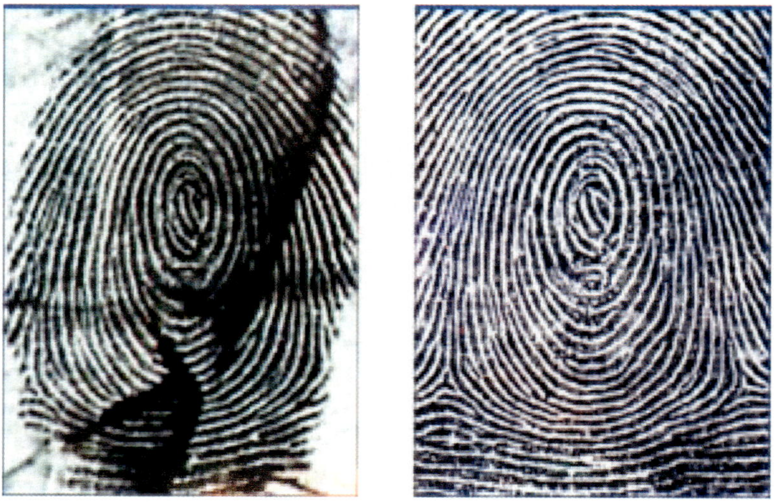

Prints with similar ridge patterns may belong to same or different fingers

At the second level of matching, it is examined whether or not the minutiae are in the same position, in the same order and have the same relationship to each other both in the known print and in the unknown impression. This type of comparison is called *coincident sequencing*. It involves determination of qualitative and quantitative likeness of the ridge characters in the two fingerprints.

Qualitative likeness implies that the minutiae of the same type must be present at exactly the same locations in two fingerprints. Quantitative likeness refers to the minimum number of ridge characters that can be identified as having qualitative likeness, in order to infer that the two impressions were made by the same finger. The quantitative likeness standard varies from one nation to another. In India, the legal requirement is the quantitative likeness of a minimum of eight minutiae.

For example, the following figure, an enlargement of a part of a fingerprint, shows eleven ridge characters. Minutiae 1, 2, 4 and 5 are ridge terminations; 3 and 9 are islands; 6 is a lake; 7 is a short independent ridge; and 8, 10 and 11 are bifurcations (see, p.18).

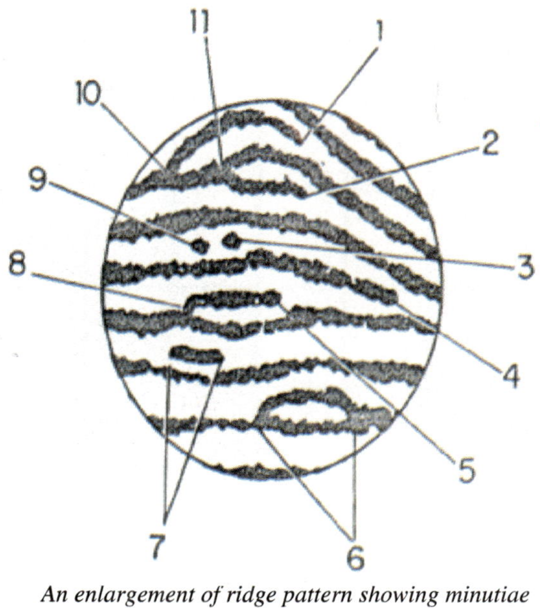

An enlargement of ridge pattern showing minutiae

According to the Indian law, if at least eight of these show qualitative likeness to the ridge characters of another fingerprint, then the two impressions belong to the same fingers. If the quantitative likeness is less than eight, then the impressions are considered as belonging to different fingers.

The coincident sequencing is generally carried out by *Osborn grid method.* In this method photographic enlargements of the developed and inked prints are prepared. One grid of equally-sized squares is superimposed on the developed print and another, exactly similar grid, is superimposed on the inked print. The squares of each grid should occupy identical positions on the two prints. An Osborn grid is shown in below.

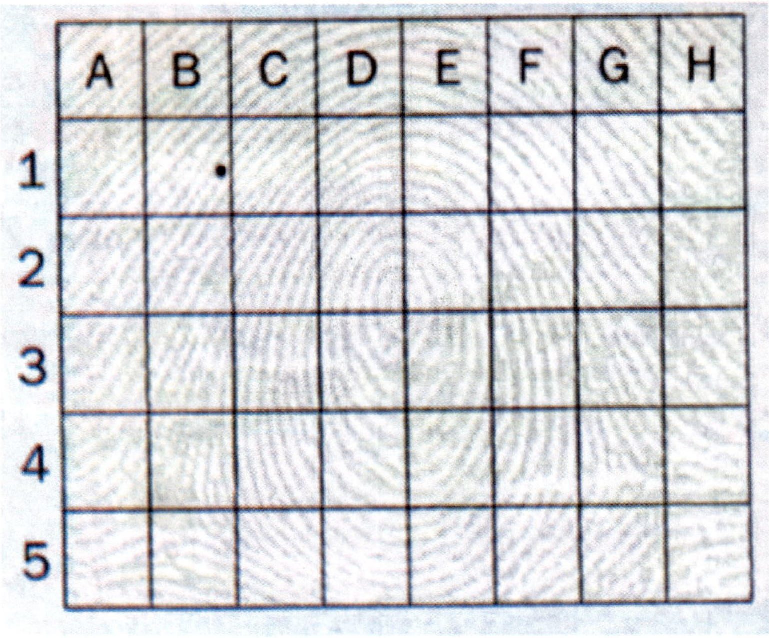

An Osborn grid

Both the prints are then examined, square for square, and the qualitative and quantitative likeness of minutiae are noted.

Figure (A), shown below, is a part of the address of a U.S.based organization, while figure (B) is a portion of a piece of art published in an Indian magazine.

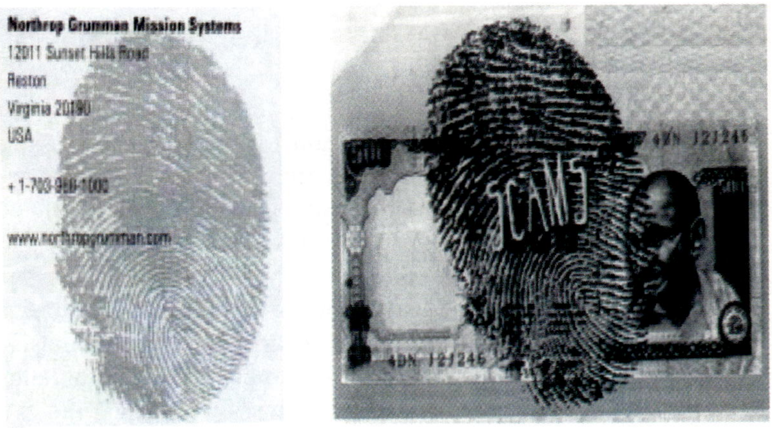

(A) (B)

A fingerprint superimposed on (A) address of an organization and (B) a piece of art

A fingerprint is superimposed on both miscellanea. Coincident sequencing shows that the two impressions were made by the same finger.

There is one in 6.4×10^{10} chance that eight characters in one finger will bear qualitative and quantitative likeness to eight characters in another finger. And the world's human population is 6.8×10^{9} – almost one-tenth of this figure!

Classification Formula for Cataloguing Fingerprints

NORMALLY, ALPHABETICAL order is followed to classify a specific commodity. For example, the books in a library are catalogued in alphabetical order with respect to the name of the author or the title of the text or both. It takes just a few minutes to pick out a particular manuscript from a bulk running into lakhs. The alphabetical order, however, does not work when criminal record is to be classified. The criminals have a large number of aliases. Moreover, the criminal record cannot be supported by photographs since by changing the dress code, hair style or religion, one can

What you see in this picture are not three criminals, but one master criminal in three disguises. Appearance can be changed, but fingerprints cannot be altered. Hence the maxim, faces may lie, fingerprints never (courtesy: National Crime Records Bureau, New Delhi)

easily change appearance.

Even before the method for fingerprint classification was devised, the experts were consentient that indexing based on a mathematical expression alone would be workable.

For deriving the mathematical expression for fingerprint classification, one has to start with the premise that fingerprint patterns fall into three broad groups: Arches, loops and whorls. On analyzing the patterns of several thousand persons, it is observed that nearly 5% fingers have arch pattern, 60% have loop pattern

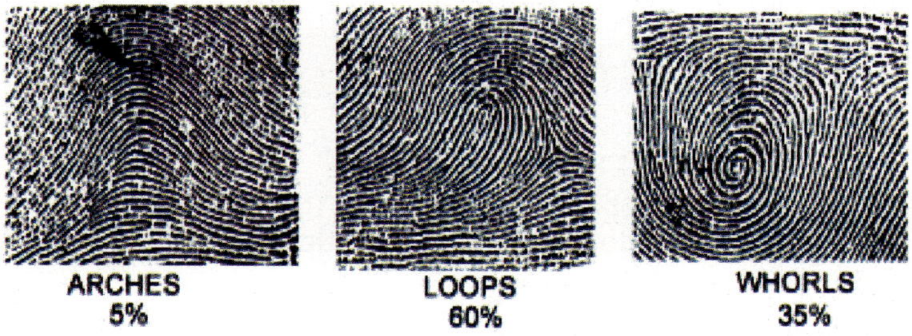

The classification formula is derived on the basis of fingerprint patterns on a person's hands

and 35% have whorl pattern.

Since statistically too few fingers have arch design, this pattern is combined with loops. Now there are two categories of finger ridges.

Loops (including arches): *L*

Whorls: *W*

Next, the ten fingers are grouped into five pairs, as shown.

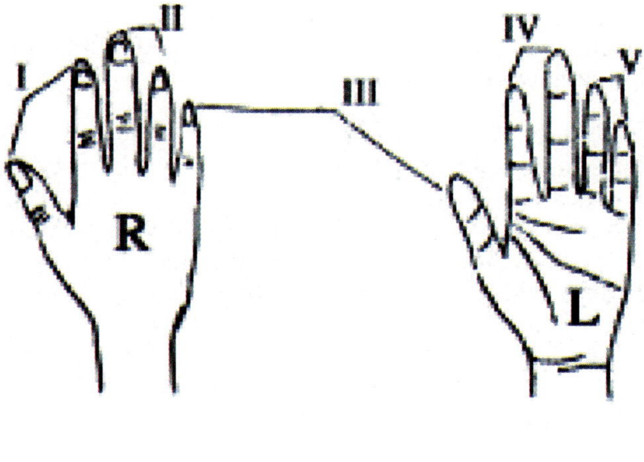

For the purpose of classification, the ten fingers are grouped into five pairs

The right hand (R) is placed left with palm down, while the left hand (L) is placed right with palm up. The pairs are arranged in the following fraction forms.

Pair	I	II	III	IV	V
Fraction	$\frac{\text{Right index}}{\text{Right thumb}}$	$\frac{\text{Right ring}}{\text{Right middle}}$	$\frac{\text{Left thumb}}{\text{Right little}}$	$\frac{\text{Left middle}}{\text{Left index}}$	$\frac{\text{Left little}}{\text{Left ring}}$

In the first pair, consisting of right index and right thumb, there are four possibilities.

a. Right index is *L*, right thumb is *W*.

b. Right index is *W*, right thumb is *L*.

c. Both are *L*.

d. Both are *W*.

These four possibilities exist in all the other pairs as well. Therefore, total number of possibilities are,

$$4 \times 4 \times 4 \times 4 \times 4 = 1024$$

The figure 1024 is the square of 32, that is,

$$32 \times 32 = 1024$$

The criminal record room has 32 cabinets (numbered 1 to 32) and each cabinet contains 32 files (numbered 1 to 32).

Whorls occurring in the 1st, 2nd, 3rd, 4th and 5th pairs are accorded a value of 16, 8, 4, 2 and 1, respectively. Loops (including arches) are assigned a value of zero, irrespective of the pair in which they occur.

We now take example of a convict whose right thumb, right ring, left middle, left index and left ring fingers have whorl patterns *(W)*, and the remaining have loop patterns *(L)*. The filing formula may be worked out as follows.

Pair	I	II	III	IV	V
Fraction	$\frac{L}{W}$	$\frac{W}{L}$	$\frac{L}{L}$	$\frac{W}{W}$	$\frac{L}{W}$
Numerical value	$\frac{0}{16}$	$\frac{8}{0}$	$\frac{0}{0}$	$\frac{2}{2}$	$\frac{0}{1}$
Add	$\frac{10}{19}$				
Further add $\frac{1}{1}$	$\frac{11}{20}$				

The fingerprints of this person would be found in the *11th file* of the *20th cabinet.*

The unit increase in the numerator and the denominator is meant to bring into the ambit of classification, a person whose all ten fingers have loop patterns. In such a case, the formula would work out to be 0/0. This would not find a place in the record room, for the cabinets and the files are numbered from 1 to 32. By adding one to the numerator and the denominator, the fraction becomes 1/1 and the fingerprint record of this person can be located in the 1st file of the 1st cabinet.

This method of cataloguing the criminal record is called *Henry System of Fingerprint Classification*, named after Sir Edward Richard Henry, former Inspector General of Police, Lower Provinces, Bengal. It was invented in India and now has worldwide application. However, the key Indian players who actually worked out this system were sidelined by the English. The ingenuity of these forgotten Indian pioneers of the science of fingerprinting and the injustice meted out to them is discussed in the next chapter.

Henry System of Classification

SIR EDWARD RICHARD HENRY was a member of Indian Civil Service and between 1873 & 1890 held various positions including the Assistant Magistrate Collector and Secretary to the Board of Revenue. It was during these postings that Henry saw a cashier taking fingerprints of labourers' while distributing their wages. This was Henry's first encounter with fingerprints. The cashier, whose name was Smith, told him that ever since the system was adopted, there had been no case of impersonation. However, the method was yet to receive the official stamp of the government.

Sir Edward Richard Henry

Henry also learnt from the cashier that Sir William Herschel – a top brass of Indian Civil Service – had, while giving a contract to a native, Rajyadhar Konai, asked him to place his right hand print on the agreement (p.17). Konai had abided by the conditions of the contract.

Henry realized that fingerprints are a perfect means of identification and may be used for classifying criminal record. He also realized that for making an attempt towards classification, sample prints running into hundreds would be required. Henry put the proposal before Herschel who, in 1891, appointed him as Inspector General of Police, with the additional charge of prisons. Data collection was now not a problem, for there were scores of prisoners under Henry's custody.

Finally a fool-proof classification system did evolve. It was based on a mathematical formula, the derivation of which we have discussed in the previous chapter. On June 12, 1897, the Council of the Governor General of India approbated that the method may be used throughout India. With passage of time all the civilized countries of the world adopted the so called *Henry System of Fingerprint Classification*.

Henry's folly

On July 12, 1900, Lord Belper, the Chairman of the Commission appointed by the Secretary of State to review the classification method asked Henry:

"Is this system an invention of your own?"
"Yes", replied Henry.

It was not.

The system was actually invented by Sub Inspectors Azizul Haque and Hem Chandra Bose, while Henry, being their superior and being an English officer, shrewdly gave his name to it.

Azizul Haque

Hem Chandra Bose

In 1899, Henry read a paper on the classification of criminal record at Dover (England) before an assembly of the British Association for the Advancement of Science. He did not acknowledge the role played by Haque and Bose in devising the system.

In 1900, the Government of India sponsored the publication of Henry's paper in enlarged form. It was entitled, *Classification and uses of Fingerprints.* Subsequently, Her Majesty's Stationery Office in England published numerous editions of the book. No word of thanks for Haque and Bose appears in any of the editions. The canniness with which Henry procured the sponsorship for the publication of this text is described in the next chapter.

Michael Carrigan, a forensic expert with Metropolitan Police, U.K. in a seminar held on September 2, 2009 advocated:

> Haque and Bose were the Indian fingerprint experts credited with primary development of the fingerprint classification system eventually named after their supervisor, Sir Edward Richard Henry.

Haque was a student of Presidency College, Calcutta where

he excelled in mathematics. In 1892, Henry requested the Principal of the college to recommend a student with a strong aptitude for statistics to work in the field of criminal identification.

The Principal nominated Haque, who was then recruited as Sub Inspector in Bengal Police.

Presidency College, Calcutta where Azizul Haque studied

Henry was never a student of mathematics. Whenever asked how he hit upon a mathematical classification formula, he used to say:

> I came up with the classification system in a sudden flash of inspiration while traveling on a

> train. I had no paper and so noted down the ideas on my shirt cuff!

Michael Carrigan further states:

> *He (Haque) devised a mathematical formula* of sorting (fingerprint) slips in 1024 pigeonholes in thirty two columns and thirty two rows....Edward Henry was overjoyed with Haque's results, and (he) saw that they would reflect well on him and (his) career...Later on, *Henry described the new classification system as if it were his own* (italics ours).

Sir Douglas Gordon, a former Inspector General of Bengal Police held:

> ...(the classification system was) invented by the(se) two Bengali officers. The names of these two Bengali officers were Azizul Haq(ue) and Hem Chandra Bose. Henry arranged for them to explain and demonstrate this system to a committee of experts in Calcutta in March 1897 and it was decided that this system had marked advantages...

The issue of honorarium

It is alleged that Haque and Bose used to tell their confidants that Henry could not even understand the system when it was patiently explained to him. They could not have done anything beyond that. In 1900, native Sub Inspectors of Police had no channel of reprisal against a British Inspector General. Nor would a high official doubt that a junior, and that too an Indian, could file a representation against him.

However, in 1925, Haque did represent his case to the government, although the way he did can hardly be called a representation.

The whole issue arose when in 1924, Haque received the title of "Khan Bahadur" and Henry, while congratulating him, remarked,

"I wish they had at the same time given you a *jagir* (a piece of land). On his retirement as Deputy Superintendent of Police and Honorary Magistrate, Haque wrote an application dated March 3, 1925 to the Governor of Bihar and Orissa:

> Your humble memorialist's prayer is that in consideration of his loyal services, especially in the matter of the adaptation of the Finger Print System to practical use....Your Excellency's benign Government may consider your humble memorialist's case with a view to the grant of *jagir*.

Haque also stated in this letter that since he was confirmed as Deputy Superintendent of Police just a year and a half before his retirement, his pension had been cut down and therefore he was finding it difficult to maintain his position. In support of his case, Haque enclosed a clipping from *The Statesman*, dated February 28, 1925 which, in an article entitled, "Indian Affairs in London" stated, "A Muhammaden Sub-Inspector played an important and still insufficiently acknowledged part (in fingerprint classification)". It is also distressing to note that in this ten-paragraph letter, Haque refers to himself as *Your Humble Memorialist* thirteen times! This is more of an appeal than a representation.

The Government of Bihar and Orissa, where Haque served his last posting, considered the application sympathetically. However, in these provinces there was no land which the government could have possibly donated to Haque. Hence it forwarded the letter to the Government of India, stating that Haque deserved to be adequately rewarded and that in place of a *jagir*, he may be awarded an honorarium from the central fund. J.D. Sifton, Esq., C.I.E., I.C.S., Officiating Chief Secretary to the Government of Bihar and Orissa further wrote (letter No. 761 PR, dated June 15, 1925):

> Azizul Haque was....allowed to start research work upon a method of classifying finger prints, and after months of experiment *he evolved his primary classification* which convinced Sir E.R. Henry that the problem of providing an

> effective method of classifying finger prints could be solved. Thereafter the secondary and other classifications were evolved and the Khan Bahadur played an important role in their conception (italics ours).

Sifton also stated that in March 1897 Haque appeared before the committee of experts constituted at the request of Henry to test scientifically the fingerprint system. He was put to all possible tests by the committee. However, neither the Government of India nor the Government of Bengal could confirm whether Haque actually appeared before the committee.

When this letter was referred to D. Petrice, Director, Intelligence Bureau, it created an element of doubt. On July 13, 1925, Petrice wrote:

> There can be no doubt whatever that the present system of classification of finger-prints was a scientific discovery of great value and has been adopted all over the world. Whether Khan Bahadur Azizul Haque took as prominent a part in evolving it as is claimed for him is, however, a matter on which I have no information. He is not mentioned in Sir Edward Henry's own book, and in the history of the finger print system as given in the Encyclopedia Britannica, Sir E. Henry is quoted as the inventor….

It also created an element of surprise for Petrice further wrote:

> If the Khan Bahadur rendered as valuable services as are alleged as long ago as 1893, it is curious that his claims to special recognition should have been so belatedly represented.

This situation arose because so long Henry was in India he did not speak or write a word about the contribution of Indian officers to the fingerprint classification system. Petrice then referred the letter to the Government of Bengal, since Haque was with

Bengal Police when the classification formula received accreditation. L. Birley, Chief Secretary to the Government of Bengal replied back on November 30, 1925 (letter No. 4382 PI):

> The key (plate) referred to in page 73 of Sir Edward's book entitled "Classification and Uses of Finger Prints" is attributed to the Khan Bahadur and this key may have suggested the arithmetical rule for determining primary classification which is the method in use at present.

Apart from this the Government of Bengal could not shed any light on Haque's role. It therefore suggested that the case may be referred to Henry himself.

Henry endorsed the grant of honorarium to Haque. In a letter dated May 10, 1926, he wrote to P.H. Dumbel, the then Secretary of the Services and General Department, India Office:

> ...I wish to make (it) clear that, in my opinion, he (Haque) contributed more than any other member of my staff and contributed in a conspicuous degree to bringing about the perfecting of a system of classification that has stood the test of time and has been accepted by most countries.

In this letter Henry also wrote:

> As in most research enquires, results were achieved by team work.

One wonders why Henry, after a lapse of 30 years, became considerate towards Haque. It is commonly believed that two factors were responsible for the change in Henry's attitude. Firstly, Haque (and Bose too) had risen to the rank of Deputy Superintendent of Police and, was therefore in a position to assert himself. Secondly, by the 1920s, the colonial grip was becoming loose. Both may be true. However, there was another reason for Henry turning soft and, we feel, that this was more important.

Four years earlier, Henry had spoken of Haque's contribution to F.W. Duke, an officer at India Office, Whitehall. Duke, in turn, wrote a letter on January 25, 1922, to Sir Havilland Le Mesurier, Acting Governor of Bihar and Odisha in which he stated:

> *Azizul Haque devised the classification* which is now in force not only in India but practically throughout the civilized world. It may have required no exceptional talent; if not done by him, the same, or an equivalent, might have been done later by someone else, but the fact remains that it was devised by *him*, has not been superseded and its use is world-wide (italics ours).

When Henry was consulted on Haque's honorarium, a copy of this letter was also sent to him. It was now not possible for Henry to retrace his steps.

At the time of final approval of honorarium, the Home Department noted:

> It appears from the information now received that he (Haque) was Sir Edward Henry's principal helper in perfecting the scheme and that he actually *himself* devised the method of classification which is in universal use. *He thus contributed most materially* to a discovery which is of world-wide importance and has brought a great credit to the police of India (italics ours).

Bose's additional contributions

In his letter to Dumbel (dated May 10, 1926), Henry also wrote:

> In addition to being indebted to Khan Azizul Haque, I was indebted to some of his colleagues but, to what extent I cannot after the lapse of nearly 29 years specify more exactly.

However, Henry contradicted himself when consulted on Bose's contribution to the system. Four years later he wrote:

> The Rai Bahadur (Bose)….has devoted the whole of his official life to perfecting the methods by which search is facilitated and as his labours have contributed materially to the success achieved he is entitled to great credit.

This shows that all along Henry was aware of the contribution which Haque and Bose rendered to the fingerprint system, but he spoke up only when asked to do so.

The contribution of Bose to the science of fingerprinting is best summed up in a communication (No. 650 PI, dated February 5, 1929) from the Government of Bengal to the Government of India, Home Department. It stated:

> During his long service in the Bengal Bureau he (Bose) acquired unique knowledge of the science and introduced various improvements in the methods of sub-classifying finger impressions of which the following are deserving of special mention:-
>
> i. The method of comparing imperfect impressions containing only a few naked ridges.
>
> ii. The sub-classification by the numerical method.
>
> iii. The method of estimating the probability of fixing identity by the ridge characteristics.
>
> iv. The sub-classification of the accidental type.
>
> v. The improved system of indexing.
>
> vi. The introduction of a telegraphic code for finger impressions.

vii. The classification system for a single digit impression.

Going by this communication it is evident that Bose contributed more to the subject of fingerprints than Haque. This has also been indicated in a note dated February 28, 1929 recorded by P.C. Bamford of the Intelligence Bureau:

> I know Rai Hem Chandra Basu (Bose) Bahadur very well, and it would be impossible to find a stronger protagonist of the fingerprint system. His open idea was to make it a success....Hem Chandra Basu (Bose) not only *did his share in the original introduction of the finger print system* all over India, but continued, throughout his whole service, to devote himself to this particular work, and for this reason I consider that his case for an honorarium is better than that of Khan Bahadur Azizul Haque... (italics ours).

By saying so Bamford was merely corroborating the recommendations of the Government of Bengal:

> The Khan Bahadur, it is understood, was associated with this work only for a period of five years when the system was in its infancy. The Rai Bahadur has, on the other hand, been upgrudging in placing on record in his books *the result of his long experience which has contributed much to the advancement of the science* and the Governor in Council considers that an honorarium of Rs. 10,000/- might appropriately be granted to him by the Government of India. In making this recommendation His Excellency in Council is influenced by the consideration that the *officer rendered exceptional service to police administration generally, not only in India as a whole but elsewhere* (italics ours).

This recommendation was, however, turned down by the Government of India on the ground that Henry had said that Haque contributed more than any other member of his staff in perfecting the system of fingerprint classification. Hence the honorarium granted to any other officer had to be less than or equal to that awarded to Haque. Nevertheless, D. Petrice, in a note dated March 5, 1929, wrote:

> I am satisfied that he (Bose) has a clearly established claim on the generosity of the Government of India in recognition of the exceptional services which he has rendered to the Police Administration generally not only in India, but in civilized countries throughout the world. I am not so satisfied, however, that there is a case for giving him an honorarium of Rs. 10,000/-, as compared with Rs. 5,000/- previously awarded to Khan Bahadur Azizul Haque.

Had Haque not applied for the award, his efforts towards evolving the classification formula would have gone unrecognized. And had Haque not got the honorarium, even Bose would not have been rewarded. Bose received the honorarium not because he applied for it, but because Haque's case had set a precedent.

We have already cited how Haque had to plead his case for honorarium, as he was facing financial difficulties after superannuation. The fate of Bose was no different. A personal letter, dated December 6, 1929, from a former superior of Bose in the Home Department, addressed to a Deputy Secretary of Finance Department pleads that the honorarium due to Bose be released at the earliest "as the Rai Bahadur is lying in a critical state at present and needs financial assistance very badly".

Training courses

In 1898, the Government of India directed that the new system of classification be introduced throughout British India, including the provinces. Henry was assigned the duty of explaining the methodology to various bureaus. In a report (No. 1641, dated February 22, 1899) he wrote to the Chief Secretary to the Government of Bengal:

> In December (1898) I proceeded to Poona and explained to the Bombay, Central Provinces and Hyderabad assigned District Police the system of classification, and in January (1899) went to Allahabad and explained the system to the North-west Provinces and Punjab Police. At both places a considerable number of finger impression slips were classified by *me* as a nucleus for their records, and all the officers who attended acquired a fair working knowledge of necessary details. During the course of next month, the system will be explained to the Burma and Madras Police, so that by the end of March the order of Government of India will have been given effect... (italics ours).

Henry submitted this report to the state government of Bengal probably because he was holding the additional charge of prison (jails are a state subject). Otherwise, being Inspector General of Police, Henry was responsible to the Central Government's Home Department. He, therefore, presented a report (No. 100 CI, dated March 23, 1899) to the Secretary to the Government of India, Home Department, where he is more precise:

> I had with me at Poona, Allahabad and Rangoon, two native assistants *who* were employed in classifying the accumulated slips. At each place *they* classified between 1,000 and 1,200 slips, and *I* verified their work. These slips now form a nucleus for the finger impression records of these provinces.....

Henry was a senior officer and therefore it is not surprising that he had two natives to assist him. However, this raises further questions. Why was the help rendered by the natives not acknowledged in the report to the state government? Why have the names of the assistants not been mentioned? Who were these assistants? One of them was certainly Bose. While making a case for grant of honorarium to Bose, J.B. Blair, Esq., I.C.S., Deputy Secretary to the Government of Bengal wrote the following note to the Secretary, Government of India, Home Department:

> The Rai Bahadur received his early training in the finger print system direct from Sir Edward Henry whom he accompanied to various provinces in India for the purpose of establishing finger print bureaux.

As an accompaniment to this report, Henry presented a list of officers who were trained in the classification method. The list is reproduced in the Table.

List of officers who received training in classification system

Region	**Names of officers**
Bombay Presidency	H. Kennedy, *Inspector General Police* Brewin, *Personal Asst. to I.G.P.* Guider, *Asst. Supt. Police* Noel, *In-charge Anthropometric Branch* *Eight Native Officers*
Madras	H.A. Stenart, *I.C.S., I.G.P.* L.G. Arbuthnot, *Deputy I.G.P.* F. Fawcett, *Dist. Supt. Police* H.D. Robertson, *Dist. Supt. Police* *Four Native Officers*
Central Provinces	One European Inspector *One Native Inspector*
Hyderabad	One European Officer

Burma	Colonel Peele, *I.G.P.* Dixon, Deputy *I.G.P.* Greenstreet, *Dist. Supt. Police* McDonnell, *Dist. Supt. Police* Snadden, *Dist. Supt. Police* Lloyd, *Dist. Supt. Police* Ingle, *Dist. Supt. Police* Skinner, *Dist. Supt. Police* Sherman, *Asst. Supt. Police* Trotter, *Asst. Supt. Police* Comber, *Asst. Supt. Police* Summers, *Asst. Supt. Police* McFurlane, *Asst. Supt. Police* Llyod, *Inspector* Havelock, *Inspector* Pedler, *Inspector* *Eight Native Officers*
North-West Provinces	J.B. Thomson, *I.C.S., I.G.P.* Greerson Jackson, *I.C.S.* C. Knyvett, *Deputy I.G.P.* C.J. Hoskins, *Dist. Supt. Police* H. Innes, *Dist. Supt. Police* D.M. Straight, *Dist. Supt. Police* F.G. Fox, Asst. Supt. Police Porter, *Asst. Supt. Police* Adams, *Asst. Supt. Police* Maloney, *Asst. Supt. Police* Fawkes, *Asst. Supt. Police* Naylor, *Asst. Supt. Police* Cameron, *Asst. Supt. Police* *Several Native Officers*
Punjab	Turton Smith, *I.G.P.* Rundle, *Dist. Supt. Police* *Two Native Officers*

The list mentions the names and designations of the English officers of each province. However, as far as Indian officers are concerned, the schedule only mentions their number. No doubt, in those days promotional avenues for Indians were limited. Yet a few of them did rise to higher ranks and those were the ones to receive training. After all, one does not expect a constable to be sitting on the same conference table where an Inspector General is occupying a chair. Moreover, the natives are mentioned as *officers* and not *personnel.* They must have been at least of the rank of Inspectors. The English Inspectors were mentioned by name, but not their Indian counterparts.

This shows the bias that Henry had towards Indians. In fact, Henry wrote in his biography that he was too big for India. This is a dignified way of saying that Indians are too small before me.

Henry's Fingerprint Treatise

WE HAD STATED in the previous chapter that the Government of India sponsored the publication of Henry's book entitled, *Classification and uses of Fingerprints* in 1900. Subsequently, Her Majesty's Stationery Office in England published numerous editions of the book.

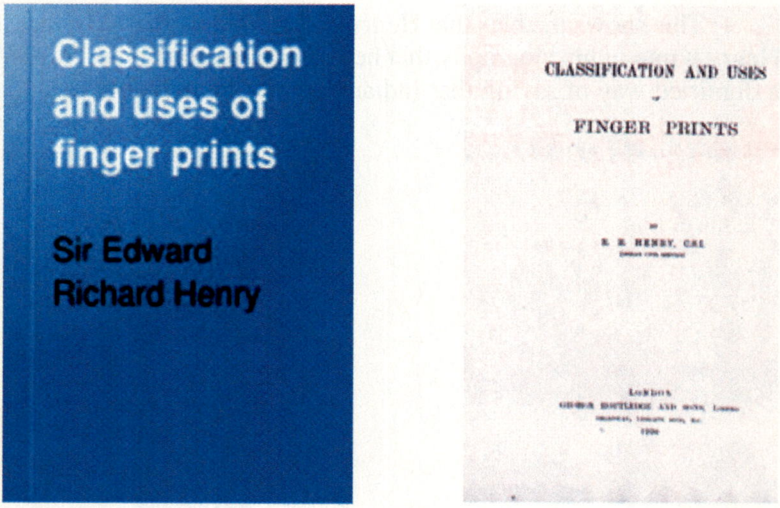

Cover page of Henry's text

Henry acted shrewd for gaining the sponsorship for the publication of this treatise. He submitted a synopsis of the proposed book and then proceeded to England on a nine months leave, commencing March 25, 1899. As is customary, the synopsis was forwarded to an independent referee, one Denzil Ibbetson, for review.

On August 12, 1899, C.W. Bolton, Chief Secretary to the Government of Bengal wrote a demi-official letter to A.H.L. Fraser, Officiating Secretary to the Government of India, Home Department, regarding the fate of the book:

> It is believed that Mr. Henry, who is now on *furlough*, intends to prepare, or is actually preparing, such a work (a manual of the system of identification by finger impressions). He has been written to, but his reply has not yet been received.....He has taken with him the blocks from which the plates to illustrate the classification and identification of the impressions can be printed...

These illustrations, some of which are shown below were official documents. If an officer working in a non-sensitive Department, such as Urban Affairs or Travel & Tourism proceeds on leave and carries some official papers with him, he is likely to face strict action. But here is an officer, working in the sensitive Home Department, who goes on a long leave to a distant land and carries with him the printing material in anticipation that the reviewer would clear his book-writing project. The government is aware of this, yet no action is taken against him.

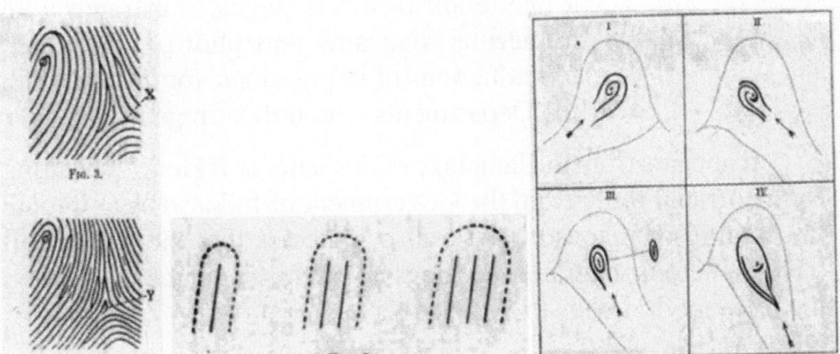

Some of the illustrations which Henry allegedly took with him to England

In response to the above letter, H. Luson, a Deputy Secretary under Fraser wrote the following note on August 30, 1899:

> Mr. Bolton may be asked to let us know Mr. Henry's reply when received. (Mr. Henry is rather given to monopolizing information on

> this subject; it is somewhat doubtful whether he will return to India).

The statement in parenthesis seems to be the personal view of Luson, but it throws light on Henry's character.

Meanwhile, Fraser traced the report of Ibbetson and on August 30, 1899, wrote the following note:

> Honourable member will see that Mr. Ibbetson ... suggests that Mr. Henry is not a suitable man to write the manual.

Finally, on October 11, 1899, Henry wrote a demi-official letter to Fraser:

> Two or three years ago I published mainly for the use of the police, a small pamphlet intended to assist those whose business it is to take and compare finger impressions. The information in this pamphlet is already out of date...I can now, if the Government of India desire, prepare a handbook of a few pages, illustrated with numerous diagrams and photo-zinographic reproductions of impressions, for the use of all the Departments who utilize finger prints.

It appears from the language of this letter as if Henry is waiting for an official reply from the Government of India so as to initiate the writing of manuscript. He also indicates that the book shall have numerous diagrams, but does not mention that he has carried the relevant drawings to England.

Fraser was soon to be replaced by J.P. Hewett as the Secretary to the Government of India, Home Department. Hewett noticed that since Henry had in his possession most of the papers concerning the publication of the book, it was imperative that he be granted the sponsorship. However, there was one stumbling block: the adverse comments of the referee. He, therefore, wrote to Ibbetson on December 6, 1899:

> Mr. Henry has information which he has not published and which no one else has. I don't think that a manual prepared by anyone else would be up to date, and I feel sure that, if we did make the work over to anyone else, Mr. Henry would not give assistance, and I hardly see how he could be asked to do so.
>
> My own opinion is that he should be entrusted with the duty of preparing a handbook as he suggests.

Mark the government's dilemma. An officer carries away the information without which the book cannot be published. In case the government thinks of granting sponsorship to someone else, he refuses to cooperate. Once again this sheds light on the type of person that Henry was.

In response to the above letter, Ibbetson wrote:

> I agree that no other course is possible, *though I despair of getting what is wanted from him* (italics ours).

Hewett could not have expected a better response. By saying neither a concrete *Yes* nor a firm *No*, Ibbetson had put the ball in the government's court – an opportunity Hewett was waiting for. He wrote to Her Majesty's Under Secretary of State for India (letter No. 5, dated January 11, 1900):

> I am directed to intimate, for the information of the Right Honourable the Secretary of State, that Mr. E.R. Henry, C.S.I., I.C.S., Inspector General of Police, Bengal, at present on *furlough* in England, has been authorized to prepare a hand-book of instructions for the classification of finger impressions. I am to request that any printing charges that Mr. Henry may incur in connection with the preparation of the hand-book may be paid by the India Office.

On the same day he wrote to Henry (Demi-official No. 18-D, dated January 11, 1900):

> In reply to your demi-official letter dated 11th October 1899, I am desired to say that the Government of India has sanctioned your proposal to prepare a handbook of instructions for the classification of finger impressions, with the necessary illustrations, in the manner indicated in your letter. The India Office is being addressed with a view to its meeting any printing charges which you may incur.

Thus the Secretary to the Government of India was forced to bend to Henry's desire. And the world knows that Henry was honored by the sponsorship granted by the Government of India for publishing the handbook on fingerprints.

Telegraphic Code System

BESIDES INVENTING the fingerprint classification formula, Hem Chandra Bose also worked out a telegraphic code system for fingerprints, which was later adopted by Scotland Yard, without acknowledging the contribution of the original innovator.

The telegraphic code served to communicate the fingerprints of a suspect from one crime record office to another at a rapid pace.

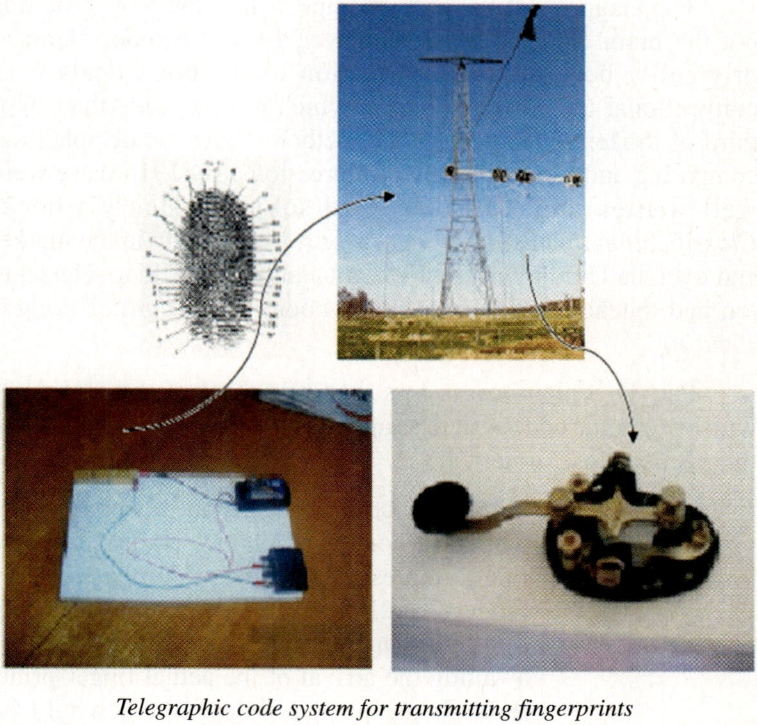

Telegraphic code system for transmitting fingerprints

Bose described the system in a book entitled, *Hints on Finger-Prints with a Telegraphic Code for Finger Impressions*, published by Messers Thacker Spink and Company in 1916 and, as far as we are aware, this is the first book on telegraphic code system for fingerprints.

In the preface Bose modestly writes:

> In offering this book to the public I do not lay any claim to originality or authority nor do I wish to infer that my abilities are above the average. The information contained in the following pages is the result of careful study combined with an experience extending over twenty years in one of the principal Finger-Print Bureaux in India.

The language of the preface implies as if the new system is not the brain child of Bose. However, Bose precludes claim to originality because a larger section of the book deals with conventional topics. Thus Part I, which covers more than two-third of the text, incorporates the methodologies for deciphering, comparing and recording finger impressions. By 1916 these were well written and well discussed subjects. Henry's book, *Classification and uses of Fingerprints*, was already in the market and even its Urdu translation was available. Sir William Herschel too had touched these topics in his book, *The Origin of Finger-Printing*.

Part II, which covers less than one-third of the text deals with telegraphic code system as applied to fingerprints. Concerning this section Bose writes:

> Part II, which is a novelty in this book, deals with a method by which the details of a man's finger impressions can be *telegraphed* to any Finger-Print Bureau for search, thus avoiding the delay inseparable from the method of awaiting the arrival of the actual finger-prints through the post, a delay which would be considerable in the case of a reference to Scotland Yard or a Colonial Bureau (italics original).

Thus Bose contends that there is novelty in the system of telegraphic code. Yet one feels that Bose could have been, rather should have been, more expressive about his invention. However, the shadow of the colonial rule and the authority of colonial officers seem to loom large over him. Bose dedicates the book to an English officer, F.C. Daly, Deputy Inspector General of Police, Crime and Railways, "To whom I express my sincere thanks for the honour of permitting me to inscribe the following pages". Thus Bose had to seek permission of his English masters to write the book and that explains his submissiveness.

We also feel that Bose, who had risen from ranks, would not have possessed a good command over English language. This must have been an additional reason for his dependence on and his submissiveness to the English officers. In fact, he writes a special word of thanks for A.E. O'Sullivan, an assistant to F.C. Daly, for reading through the proofs of his book!

Home Department Records reveal that Bose's publisher sent a copy of the book to the Chief Secretary to the Government of India along with a covering letter, dated September 14, 1917, which read as follows:

> The author has asked us to solicit the patronage of your Government for the book should you consider it of value. We may mention that the Government of Bengal have included it in the list of "Works of Utility" and it is having a very large sale.

The Chief Secretary* replied back to the publisher on October 23, 1917:

> The book is brief and simple and should be useful to beginners...but I do not see how the Home Department can patronize it. That may be left, I think, to local governments and police officers.

---

* The Chief Secretary had signed this letter without putting his name below the signatures, as is the normal practice. The signatures are not legible and therefore we could not identify the name of the Chief Secretary.

The Chief Secretary's refusal to patronize the book seems reasonable. However, it is clear that he did go through the text. He finds no objection to Bose's statement that Part II is a novelty. It is also reasonable to conclude that the Government of Bengal included the text in the list of "Works of Utility" because it dealt with the telegraphic code system. Otherwise, as has been stated earlier, there were quite a few books on conventional aspects of fingerprint technique.

The method devised by Bose was cost-effective, as he states in the foreword:

> It is with a view to reducing as far as possible (this) inevitable delay before the antecedents of strangers and suspicious characters can be known after their finger impressions have been taken, that this code for telegraphing details of finger impressions at a cost which is not prohibitive has been compiled.

The first English officer to recognize the utility of telegraphic code for fingerprinting was Sir Charles Stockley Collins, Detective Superintendent, Scotland Yard. His book, *A Telegraphic Code for Fingerprint Formulae*, was published in 1921 – five years after Bose's publication. This was stated by P.C. Bamford of the Intelligence Bureau, while recommending the honorarium for Bose. In a note dated February 28, 1929, he wrote :

> Hem Chandra Basu (Bose) published his code in 1916, and … it has been used in the Bengal Bureau since 1917. Mr. Collins of Scotland Yard published a telegraphic code in 1921, and, in his preface, mentioned that his treatise was originally written some seven years previously. Since he did not publish it till 1921, I think that Rai Hem Chandra Basu Bahadur can claim to be the first in the field with a practical finger print telegraphic code.

Sir Charles Stockley Collins

Once the government cleared the honorarium for Bose, a request was made to the Standing Finance Committee to release the grant. S.N. Roy, Esq., I.C.S., Deputy Secretary, Home Department, in a note dated July 8, 1929, wrote:

> This (telegraphic code) was a work involving arduous labour and although Scotland Yard published a similar telegraphic code in 1921 it is noteworthy that the Rai Bahadur's work was the first of its kind.

Collins pointed out that any recognition made solely by coded information would only supply a "strong suspicion", which had to be confirmed by comparison of the actual finger impression. This is exactly what Bose wrote five years earlier:

> It is of course intended that in practical working the actual finger-prints would follow by post in confirmation of the telegram.

It also seems that Indians had been working on the telegraphic code system much earlier than the English officers had any idea of it. In the preface of his book, Bose writes:

> The portion regarding the *minutiae* coding has been taken, with a slight modification, from a draft code roughly drawn up in 1903 by Inspector N.C. Mukerjee of the Bengal Police, to whom my thanks are (also) due (italics original).

After the publication of Collins book, Scotland Yard adopted the new system. In 1924, it solved the first case using the telegraphic code method. Thereafter, many other cases must have been solved by application of the code system. However, no one remembered, or gave credit to, Bose – the original inventor of the technique.

Single Digit Classification System

THE IDEA of fingerprint code system, as described in the previous chapter was to transmit, at a very fast pace, the finger impressions of an alleged criminal from one bureau to another. However, it was not practical to telegraph all ten imprints of the person in question. Therefore, Bose modified the existing fingerprint classification formula, which was based on the ridge pattern of all ten digits. Against this, he devised a classification formula based on single finger impressions.

Index finger Impression of…..

A single fingerprint index card

At the Scotland Yard, Sir Charles Stockley Collins made an attempt to devise a single digit classification system. However, he did not consider each finger as being independent of the others.

Had he done so, perhaps a simple classification method would have evolved. Instead, what resulted was an extremely tedious procedure for filing single digit index cards. For this reason, the classification method devised by Collins was subsequently abandoned.

In June 1926, Harry Battley took over as Head of the Fingerprint Department of the Yard. With the assistance of Detective Sergeant Frederick Rupert Cherrill he tried to remove the drawbacks inherent in the Collins classification method. The duo dissected a conventional fingerprint index card into ten independent collections, one for each digit. During 1928-29, they classified a few hundred slips according to the new method. In 1930, Battley's book, *Single Fingerprints*, was published by Her Majesty's Stationery Office.

Harry Battley

Battley perhaps did not realize that he had already been superseded in this endeavor by Bose, who had not only worked out the single digit classification formula much earlier, but had also got it published.

In an Intelligence Bureau note dated February 28, 1929, P.C. Bamford wrote:

> I place below my own copy of the "Finger Print Companion", which I believe to be his (Bose's) latest work. The interesting portion(s) of this book relate(s) to the classification of single digit impressions.....

Finger Print Companion was published by Gaudiya Printing Works, Calcutta in 1927 – three years before Battley's publication. Bose's earlier book, *Hints on Finger-Prints with a Telegraphic Code for Finger Impressions*, had become so popular that there was a persistent demand to bring out its 2nd edition. In *Finger Print Companion*, Bose incorporated both the newly discovered system of single digit classification and the reprinted version of *Hints on Finger-Prints with a Telegraphic Code for Finger Impressions*. He believed that the combined text would serve as a ready reference on fingerprints. In the preface Bose writes:

> I regret the delay in meeting the demands for my *Hints on Finger Prints* by getting up a fresh edition earlier, as I was engaged for some time in making researches in connection with the classification of a single digit or *chance* impression for the purpose of identifying persons who may have unknowingly left any impression when handling various articles, such as, glass, paper, polished wood, china ware &c. It is impossible to express adequately my appreciation of the generous support by Courts, Lawyers and the Police...I trust this new book...will answer the purpose of a ready book of reference (italics original).

Just how interesting or useful the text was may be gauged by the fact that in the February 28, 1929 note of Intelligence Bureau, referred to above, an assistant of Bamford (one Mr. Singh) had scribbled in the margin that the Home Department may kindly return the book after review. Bamford further wrote:

> The value of a single print classification is immense from the point of view of the detection of a crime in which only the prints of one or two fingers have been left by the criminal, and I understand that the Bengal Bureau have, for some time past, been classifying finger prints by this method.

In the opinion column of his book, Bose solicited comments from a few English police officers. Most noteworthy is that of J.E. Armstrong, Deputy Inspector General of Police, Bengal, who wrote:

> If the Rai Bahadur has indeed made this new discovery in the science of identification by fingerprints, as I believe he has, it will be one more triumph for him and perhaps his greatest.

While sanctioning the honorarium for Bose, the Standing Finance Committee, during its proceedings of August 6, 1929, recorded:

> During his long service in the Bengal Finger Print Bureau he (Bose) acquired a unique knowledge of the science and introduced various improvements which had been of great use to the police administration not only in India but throughout the world. Particular mention might be made of the system of classification for a single digit impression which had been acknowledged to be a master piece of finger print work by many experts in Europe....

J.R. Blair, Esq., I.C.S., Deputy Secretary to the Government of Bengal, while making a case for rewarding Bose, wrote to the Secretary, Government of India, Home Department (letter No. 650 PI, dated February 5, 1929):

> The utility of the system of classifying single digit impressions is obvious as it answers to all the conventional standards of proof held by experts as essential for identification. The system has been put to practical test in the Finger Print Bureau and has been found to be reliable. This achievement has been acknowledged to be a master piece of finger print work by many European experts and a reference was made to it in the "International Public Safety" dated the 30th September 1925, the official journal of the International Police Commission of Europe.

The journal, *International Public Safety*, a publication of International Criminal Police Commission, in its September 30, 1925 issue, reviewed the proceedings of the International Police Exhibition, held in June 1925 at Karlsruhe, Baden (Germany). Regarding Bose, the Government Councillor of Germany's Ministry of Interior wrote:

> Rai Bahadur Hem Chandra Bose... recently published a new method for the classification of a single digit impression which, it seems to me, as worth of special attention....Although it was not possible to present the new method at the International Police Exhibition arranged at Karlsruhe in June last, yet the closer connection formed on the occasion of this exhibition between the police administration of India and Baden offered an opportunity of acquainting wider circles of experts with his method.

A part of the reprint of International Public Safety, highlighting the contribution of Bose, is reproduced here.

ité Publique Internationale — Journal officiel ...mmission internationale de police criminelle

International Public Safety — Official Journal of the International Criminal Police Commission

Pubblica Sicurezza Internazionale — Giornale ufficiale per le comunicazioni della Commissione internazionale di polizia criminale

Schriftleiter — Rédacteur en chef — Editor — Redattore: Hofrat Dr. Oskar Dressler

...tion et administration: Vienne, I., Schottenring 11 — Office: Vienna, I., Schottenring 11 — Redazione ed amministrazione: Vienna, I., Schottenring 11

Bezugspreis ganzjährig — Abonnement annuel — Subscription yearly — Abbonamento annuale: 55 Schweizer Franken.

...t am 15. und letzten jeden Monates. — Paraît le 15 et le dernier de chaque mois. — Appears on the 15th and on the last of every month. — Esce il 15 e l'ultimo d'ogni mese.

...rgang — Wien, 30. September 1925 — Nr. 18

...druck aller Artikel sowie die ...e von Bildern ist nur mit Ge...ng der Schriftleitung gestattet. | La reproduction de tous les articles ainsi que des portraits est permise seulement avec le consentement de la Rédaction. | The reproduction of both paragraphs and portraits is permitted only with the consent of the Editorial Board. | La riproduzione di tutti gli articoli e quella delle fotografie è soltanto permessa col consenso della Redazione.

...ur Frage der Einfingerkartei.

...s Klassifizierungsverfahren von Einzelfingerabdrücken.

...ungsrat **Jung** im Ministerium des Innern, Karlsruhe (Baden).

...dem Titel „Classification of a Single Digit ...“ hat der Leiter des Erkennungsdienstes in ... zugleich Sachverständiger für Fingerabdruck... der Provinz Bengalen, Superintendent Rai ... Chandra Bose, bekannt durch seine Schrift ... Finger Prints“, vor kurzem ein neues Ver... die Klassifizierung des Einzelfingerabdruckes ...cht, das mir ganz besonderer Beachtung wert ...

...n modernen erkennungsdienstlichen Zentralen ...l neben der allgemeinen Fingerabdruckkartei ...rklassifizierung) noch eine Einfingerkartei, ins... der Einbrecher, geführt. Diese beschränkt sich ...sammlung von Einzelfingerabdrucken, geordnet ...ster und Linienanzahl, ohne weitere Unter...ung.

Autour de la question des cartes à un doigt.

Nouveau procédé de classification des empreintes d'un seul doigt.

Par le conseiller de gouvernement **Jung** du Ministère de l'intérieur à Karlsruhe (Bade).

Sous le titre „Classification of a Single Digit Impression“, le chef du service d'identité à Calcutta, en même temps expert délégué pour les rapports sur les empreintes digitales dans la province du Bengale, le surintendant Rai Sahib Hem Chandra Bose, connu par sa brochure „Hints on Finger Prints“, a récemment publié un nouveau procédé de classification des empreintes à un seul doigt qui me semble mériter une attention toute spéciale.

Dans les bureaux modernes, où les services d'identité sont concentrés, on trouve bien, en dehors du casier général d'empreintes digitales (classification à dix doigts), aussi un casier pour les empreintes à un seul doigt, particulièrement pour celles des cambrioleurs. Toutefois, ce dernier se borne à rassembler les empreintes, en les rangeant suivant le dessin et le nombre des lignes, sans ...

On the Question of a Single Digit Card-Index.

A New Method of the Classification of Single Digit Impressions.

By Government Councillor **Jung** of the Ministry of the Interior Karlsruhe, Baden.

Under the title "Classification of a Single Digit Impression" Superintendent Rai Sahib Hem Chandra Bose, Director, Identification Service of Calcutta, and also an expert of the Province of Bengal for advisory opinions on finger prints, who is well known by his publication "Hints on Finger Prints", recently published a new method for the classification of a single digit impression which, it seems to me, is worth of special attention.

It is true, in the modern central offices for the identification of persons a card-index of one finger prints, especially in the case of burglars, is kept in addition to to the general card-index of finger prints (ten fingers classification), but such card-index is confined to the collection of single digit impressions, arranged according to patterns and the number of lines, without any further secondary classification being made.

The September 30, 1925 issue of International Public Safety highlighted Bose's endeavor in working out single print classification method (Courtesy: INTERPOL, Lyon, France)

Bose was nominated as Honorary Member of the Police Exhibition Committee. It was during this event that many European experts came to know about the single digit classification method. It is quite obvious that Scotland Yard would have been represented at the exhibition. The officer(s) would have noted that Bose was able to classify single digit impressions because, unlike Collins, he treated each digit as differentia. This central idea has also been highlighted in *Finger Print Companion*, wherein Bose writes:

> For the purpose of search under this method in the records of the finger-print bureaux where the impression slips are classified and arranged under the Henry system of 10 digit classification, each of the 10 digit impressions on the record slips is to be classified separately under the single digit system....

Battley and Cherrill started working on single digit classification about a year after the police exhibition. The tip-off on digit segregation would have guided them in this endeavor.

Thus while Collins was groping in the dark and Battley and Cherrill were yet to enter the scene, Bose had smartly worked out the classification formula for the single digit impressions. The system had been tested in casework investigations, had been published in a book and had been held credible by an international journal. Why then Bose was not recognized as the originator of the system? We fail to understand!

Fingerprint Evidence World's First Conviction

WE HAD STATED in an earlier chapter that the very first fingerprint bureau of the world was inaugurated in Calcutta in 1897. The *Bengal Fingerprint Bureau*, as it came to be known, standardized the methods of recording, detecting, developing and preserving fingerprints. These protocols, with small or no modifications are still relevant.

The Bengal Fingerprint Bureau also secured for India – and the world – the first ever conviction on the basis of fingerprints left at a scene of crime. The case happened on August 16, 1897 when Hriday Nath Ghosh, the manager of Katalguri Tea Estate in Jalpaiguri, near the Indo-Bhutan border, was found murdered at his residence. His throat had been slit and his dispatch box and safe had been tampered with.

Katalguri tea estate

C.E. Gouldsbury, the then Superintendent of Police, Jalpaiguri, was at his dinner table when a constable brought the ill-fated news from the tea garden. Since it was a cold-blooded murder, Gouldsbury decided to personally supervise the investigations.

Early next morning, Gouldsbury's orderlies gathered camping equipment and riding two elephants they all set out on a journey that was anything but pleasant. For reaching the tea plantation, they had to traverse two forest areas.

The first one had a lofty growth of tiger grass, at places as tall as the elephants. To Gouldsbury and his men, the track they were traveling was barely visible, but the mahouts made the way unhesitatingly and with professional caliber. Several hours later they emerged out of the wild region, into a pasture of about one mile stretch. This, of course, they covered rapidly.

The entry into the second forest tract marked the final and most arduous phase of the trip. Here the growth was so thick that the mahouts had to dismount at regular intervals to relocate the correct path. On their way back they would rely more on animals' sense of smell, rather than their own sixth sense. At night, they set up their camp in the forest, lighted fires and shot several rounds of blanks to ward off wild animals.

Next morning they resumed their journey and soon arrived at a forest outpost. From here they picked up a ranger, who was to be their guide for the last ten miles span.

A few hours later, when tall trees gave way to trimmed bushes, the troop realized that they were at Katalguri plantation. For Gouldsbury it was a refreshing sight, but more soothing was the fact that an inspector from a local police post was already there, almost through with the inquiries.

The inspector found a calendar in book form in the dispatch box of the deceased. The blue cover of the calendar had two faint blood-stained fingerprints. One of these was deciphered to be a partial impression of the suspect's right hand thumb. It is shown in the figure below.

Partial thumb print of the suspect

Though the safe had been rifled, bundles of currency notes were found intact. The inspector opined that robbery was not the motive or, at least, not the only motive of crime. This turned out to be true.

The needle of suspicion pointed to a cook on whose clothes were found a few blood spots and an ex-servant, who had, a few years ago, been convicted of theft in Hriday Nath's house.

The cook alleged that the night before he had slaughtered a pigeon for his master's meals and drops of the bird's blood had splashed on his clothes. Chemical analysis of blood supported the cook's claim and delisted him as a suspect.

The ex-servant, whose name was Rajan Singh alias Kangali Charan, was earlier accused by Hriday Nath of stealing household items. He was prosecuted and subsequently imprisoned for six months. He was released just a few weeks earlier.

Gouldsbury realized that since Kangali Charan had served a prison sentence, his thumb impression must have been recorded by the jail authorities and later communicated to the fingerprint bureau. He, therefore, directed that photograph of the blood mark found on the calendar be sent for comparison to the Writers' Building, which housed the Bengal Bureau.

Kangali Charan's thumb print at criminal record office matched with that found at the murder site. Efforts were then made to trace the accused. He was finally arrested from Birbhum, about 300 miles from Katalguri plantation.

Initially, he denied his involvement in the crime. However, a piece of garment belonging to Hriday Nath was found in his possession. Before fleeing the scene of crime, he had picked up the victim's cloth. Acting smart, he had cut off the portion bearing the washerman's mark. When questioned, he alleged that the torn part of the overall had got burnt. However, the fabric did not show any sign of charring.

Kangali Charan was brought to Calcutta, where his right thumb impression was recorded once more. This too matched with the blood fingermark in Hriday Nath's bedroom. It was now clear that he had murdered his former employer out of revenge. He had also decamped with a few hundred rupees from the victim's safe.

Accordingly, Kangali Charan was charged with murder and theft. On the basis of the thumb print evidence he was sentenced to two years imprisonment on charge of theft. However, he was acquitted of murder charge. At that time the law did not approve of fingerprint experts as witnesses in criminal cases. The court, therefore, refrained from using the fingerprint evidence to convict him of the larger crime.

Ninety years later, on November 22, 1986, the Indian Postal Department released a first day cover depicting the Bengal Fingerprint Bureau. It is displayed below.

Bengal Fingerprint Bureau and Kangli Charan's thumb print on a postal first day cover

Superimposed on the cover is the partial thumb impression of Kangali Charan – the first convict to be tried on the basis of fingerprint evidence.

Forgery of Fingerprints

DURING THE EARLIER years of twentieth century, the science of fingerprinting elicited a lot of excitement and interest amongst Indian professionals, including police officers, scientists, lawyers and civil servants. Even though this science was in its infancy, yet it commanded respect since a large section of the society had become aware of its being the best means of identification. However, in 1917, a demonstration by a lawyer in Howrah (Bengal) court created a quibbling that threatened to undermine the value of fingerprints.

The lawyer, Babu Panchkowry Chatterji, was then invited to Bengal Fingerprint Bureau and asked to re-demonstrate his experiment. He took a thin piece of paper, and smeared it lightly with gum arabic. He then placed it over an inked fingerprint and pressed it for 1-2 minutes. Next, he slightly wetted the paper and separated it from the original impression so that it now carried the negative of the imprint. He applied the negative to a fresh sample of paper, wetted and pressed again, and removed it, thus producing a clear replica of the original impression. The original fingerprint was not damaged in this process.

These findings made sensational news. In order to search for an antidote, the fingerprint experts targeted two parameters: Ink and paper. They found that impressions produced by aniline ink could not be transferred. However, for the purpose of recording fingerprints, it was not practical to phase out printer's ink in favor of aniline ink because the latter faded out with time, especially when exposed to sunlight. Ordinary writing ink too proved useless because its free-flow property gave smudged impressions. Attempts were made to concentrate the writing ink by adding glycerin or gum arabic. The modified ink was no doubt quite viscous but, unlike printer's ink, more susceptible to attack by chemicals.

Next, the fingerprint experts shifted their research to paper. It was found that fingerprints impinged on soft and porous paper could not be transferred. In fact, Chatterji was once again invited to the bureau and asked to transfer the inked fingerprints from such papers. He could not. However, this type of paper was useless for pen and ink calligraphy (imagine writing on a newspaper with a fountain pen). Even though the problem was not solved, a very important finding emerged. It was realized that the porous paper absorbed ink very rapidly into its capillaries, so that it became unavailable for relocation. In paper of fine quality this phenomena would occur too slowly. In fact, it was found that older prints on smooth paper were less likely to be forged.

It then occurred to F. Brewester, the then Government Examiner of Questioned Documents that if somehow the inked fingerprints were rapidly dried, the forging may be obviated. Brewester observed that application of hot iron to fresh imprints negated the transference process. In this case the ink did not seep into the fibers of the paper, but rapidly evaporated from the surface. Anyway, the purpose was served. However, this created another difficulty – this time a financial one. In those days it was not possible for the Government of India to provide an electric iron to each fingerprint bureau.

However, Brewester realized that the major problem was not to prevent tampering at the bureau, but to deal with private money lenders. It was feared that astute money lenders would implant borrowers' thumb print on fresh proforma and fill in larger principal amounts and/or higher rates of interest. This would create grave law and order problems.

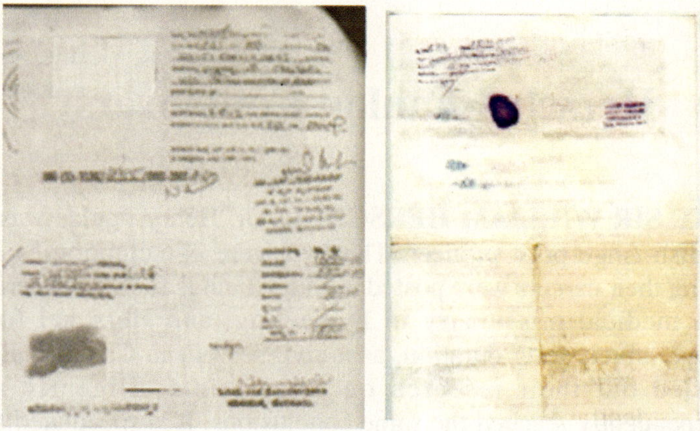

It was feared that private money lenders would tamper with financial documents

Brewester then submitted himself to a test prepared by Howrah Bar. The test consisted of 12 fingerprints – a random mix of genuine and transferred ones – on a single sheet of paper. He was asked to segregate them. In one attempt, Brewester identified the forged fingerprints. He noticed the following three differences.

1. The transferred prints had diffused lines, while the originals had sharp patterns.
2. The transferred prints were impregnated with gum.
3. The fibers on the part of paper with transferred prints were disoriented.

Brewester therefore concluded that an observant fingerprint expert can easily differentiate an original mark from a transplanted one.

Thus the matter ended.

Herschel-Faulds Controversy

LIKE SIR WILLIAM HERSCHEL, Dr. Henry Faulds was an English fingerprint pioneer. The two were contemporaries and during their careers were posted in India, Faulds for a brief period, as a medical missionary in Darjeeling, and Herschel for a comparatively long duration, as a civil servant in Calcutta. Both carried out their research on fingerprints diligently and independently reached the same conclusions. It is speculated that Faulds got interested in fingerprinting during his brief stint at Darjeeling. However, he could not get along with his superiors and soon returned to his native place, Scotland. While Herschel got all the credit for his contribution to the science of fingerprints, Faulds was marginalized, giving rise to, what in the fingerprint circles is referred to as, the Herschel-Faulds controversy.

Although none of these experts was Indian, we have incorporated the Herschel-Faulds controversy in this text for two reasons. Firstly, Herschel carried out all his fingerprint experiments while he was serving in India. Secondly, we wish to give credit to Faulds for his role in the advancement of fingerprint discipline. As stated earlier, two Indian fingerprint experts, Azizul Haque and Hem Chandra Bose, too were sidelined, much like Dr. Henry Faulds, despite their immense contribution to the subject of fingerprints.

During his postings as the Magistrate of Arrah (in 1858) and Nudded (in 1860), Herschel recorded the fingerprints of many of his British and Indian colleagues and preserved them. After a lapse of a few years, he again took their fingerprints and compared them with earlier impressions. He observed that the prints remained unchanged with time. For example, figure (A) shows the impression of Herschel's own fingerprint which he recorded in 1860, while the one shown in figure (B) is the impression of the same finger, recorded in 1888. Even after a gap of 28 years, the two prints did not reveal any difference in ridge patterns or ridge characters.

However, Herschel conducted these experiments not in his official capacity, but merely as a hobby.

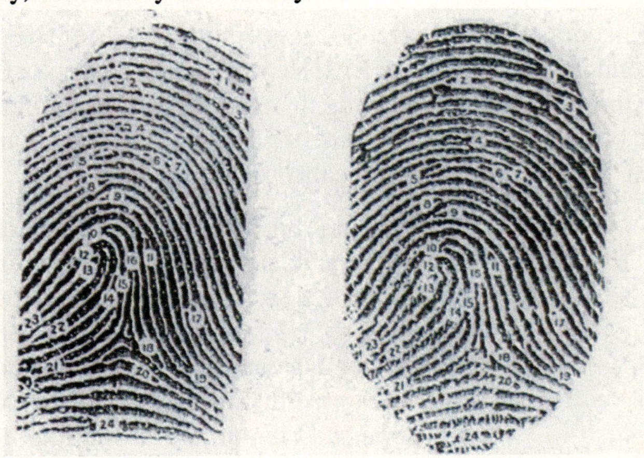

(A) (B)

Fingerprints do not change with time. Prints (A) and (B) were recorded after a gap of 28 years

In 1877 Herschel as the Magistrate and Collector at Hooghly made it mandatory on the part of the concerned individuals to put

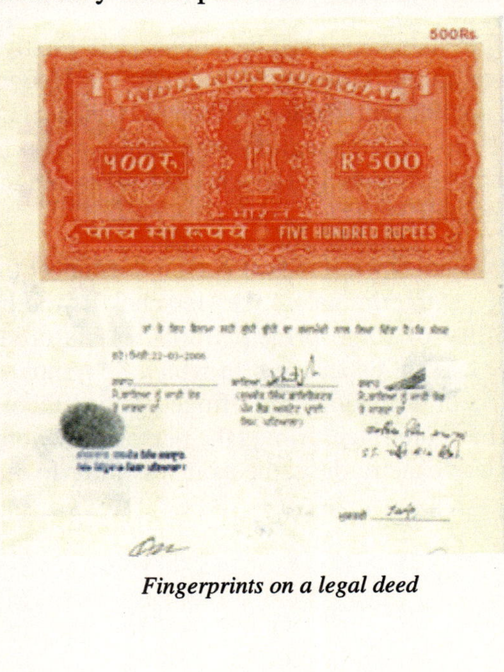

Fingerprints on a legal deed

their finger impressions on all legal deeds and financial transactions. The rule still persists.

Encouraged by the effectiveness of the new system he thought of introducing the concept in jails. He wrote to the Inspector General of Prisons in Bengal advocating that persons committed to prison should be fingerprinted to confirm their identities. This letter, dated August 15, 1877, came to be called the *Hooghly Letter*:

> It (the fingerprint system) exhibits a method of identification of persons, which with ordinary care in execution, and with judicious care in the scrutiny, is, I can now say, for all practical purposes far more infallible than photography.... I am able to say that these marks do not change in the course of ten or fifteen years so much as to affect the utility of the test....Here is a means of verifying the identity of everyman in jail with the man sentenced by the court, at any moment, day or night....Will you kindly give the matter a little patient attention, and then let me ask whether you would let me try it in other jails?

Two unfortunate facts need be emphasized. Firstly, Herschel did not receive an encouraging response to the Hooghly Letter. The reason is not difficult to trace. Although Herschel had 20 years of experience on experimentation with fingerprints, he did not publish his findings. Secondly, Herschel did not use fingerprints for identifying criminals.

Dr. Henry Faulds was the first person to connect fingerprints at crime scenes with criminals. Like Herschel, he too believed in the immutability of fingerprint patterns. He is credited with conducting a classical experiment in which he removed the skin from the fingers of his patients after fingerprinting them. After the skin re-grew, he again fingerprinted the persons and noted that the ridge pattern was exactly the same as it was prior to the removal of skin.

Dr. Henry Faulds

Around the year, 1879 when Faulds was serving as a missionary doctor in Japan, he found artifacts of prehistoric pottery bearing fingermarks of the potters. He collected several such artifacts from the beaches along the Bay of Yedo, Japan. Like Herschel, he too started collecting and examining the fingerprints of his colleagues. However, unlike Herschel, he thought of using the system for crime detection. The Japanese police sought his assistance twice to compare the fingerprints left at the scenes of crime with those of the suspects. The persons identified by fingerprints subsequently pleaded guilty.

The controversy

Faulds communicated his findings to the prestigious science journal, *Nature* for favor of publication as a letter to the editor.

The paper appeared in the October 28, 1880 issue of the journal. Entitled, *On the skin furrows of the hand*, the communication stated:

> A large number of nature-prints have been taken by me from the fingers of people in Japan, and I am at present collecting others from different nationalities, which I hope may aid students of ethnology in classification.....When bloody finger-marks of impressions on clay, glass, etc. exist, they may lead to the scientific identification of criminals. Already I have had experience in two such cases, and found useful evidence from these marks.

Herschel read Faulds' letter and responded by publishing a short communication entitled, *Skin furrows on the hand* in *Nature*, dated November 25, 1880. The Herschel-Faulds controversy stems from this date. Herschel described his experience of introducing fingerprints into various official areas:

> I have been taking sign-manuals by means of finger-marks for now more than twenty years, and have introduced them for practical purposes in several ways in India with marked benefit. The object has been to make all attempts at personating, or at repudiation of signatures, quite hopeless wherever this method is available.....I may add that by comparison of the signatures of persons now proved that much time at least makes no such material change as to affect the utility of the plan.

In October 1893, the British Government appointed Charles Edward Troup as chairman of a committee to inquire into the method of identifying habitual criminals. The committee stated that the fingerprint system had been first suggested, and to some extent applied practically, by Herschel. Faulds objected to this assertion. He wrote a letter entitled, *On the identification of habitual criminals by fingerprints* in the October 4, 1894 issue of *Nature*.

He referred to his earlier letter in *Nature* dated October 28, 1880, stating that this was the first published work on fingerprinting. He also stated that Herschel's first publication on the subject appeared a month later than his own. He further wrote:

> As priority of publication is generally held to count for something, and as I knew absolutely nothing of Sir W. Herschel's studies, nor even heard of anyone in India who did, some little evidence on the point of priority would be of interest even now.

Herschel replied through a letter entitled, *Fingerprints* published in the November 22, 1894 issue of *Nature*. He emphasized that Faulds came upon fingerprint system in 1879, while he had been making use of it since 1858. He also made a reference to the Hooghly Letter of 1877:

> I need now only add, at Mr. Faulds request, a copy of the demi-official letter which I had addressed to the then Inspector-General of Jails in Bengal. That the reply I received appeared to me altogether discouraging was simply the result of my very depressed state of health at that time.

Nothing official about it

For his contribution to the fingerprint science, the British Government decorated Herschel with knighthood. Faulds was denied this privilege. He felt all the more let down when, in 1901, Scotland Yard created a fingerprint bureau. In 1889, Faulds had approached the Scotland Yard with a proposal to open up a fingerprint bureau at his own expense. However, it is alleged that his suggestion invited rebuke from a police officer, who made insinuations regarding his sanity.

In frustration, Faulds committed a mistake. During the 1905 trial of Stratton brothers, he sided with the defence. The brothers, Alfred and Albert Stratton were accused of murdering an old couple, Thomas and Ann Farrow in their home, above their shop in London.

The residence of Farrows'

A thumb print was found on the cash box of the deceased. It had sufficiently clear ridge pattern.

Thumb impression of Alfred Stratton

The thumb impression belonged to one of the accused, Alfred. Faulds regarded the impression as smudged and expressed doubts on its validity. Nevertheless, the Stratton brothers were convicted of murder and duly hanged.

Fauld should have known, and in all probability would have known, that for identification purposes the entire fingerprint impression need not be clear. Then why did he play a negative role in the court's proceedings? No doubt, he was against Herschel and against Scotland Yard, but it was unwise to go against a system based on sound scientific doctrine, a system which had passed the acid test. By doing so, he induced the public opinion to go against him.

The Strattons case left a long lasting scar on Fauld's faculties. As late as 1954, Detective Chief Superintendent, Frederick R. Cherrill of the Scotland Yard wrote in his book, *The Fingerprint System at New Scotland Yard*:

> It is beyond doubt that Herschel was in the field many years before Faulds; in fact there is incontrovertible proof that Herschel was experimenting with finger, palm and sole prints when Faulds was but 16 years old.

However, another fingerprint specialist, John Berry, for many years editor of the reputed journal, *Fingerprint Whorld*, feels that justice has been denied to Faulds. Writing on, *The Faulds Legacy* in his journal he states:

> In Herschel's own words he was working with fingerprints twenty three years prior to Faulds *Nature* letter, consequently it was surely his responsibility to publicly announce his researches at a time convenient to himself.

Faulds died at Staffordshire, U.K. in 1930. The Japanese honored him by installing a commemorative stone at Tsukiji where he once served as a doctor. No one bothered to preserve the gravestone of Faulds. It was in a shabby state till 1987 when, as a goodwill gesture, two American fingerprint experts, James Mock and Michael Carrick, paid for its repairs. The repaired gravestone is shown below.

Dr. Henry Faulds grave at St. Margaret Churchyard, Wolstanton, U.K.

Faulds two daughters tried in vain to have a bronze bust of their father installed at the Reception Hall of the New Scotland Yard.

Recognition at last

During his lifetime, Faulds did not receive the accolade he

Henry Faulds' memorial at Beith, Scotland

deserved. Nevertheless, in late 2002, more than seventy two years after his death, Dr. Henry Faulds – Beith Commemorative Society was established to raise a memorial to this fingerprint pioneer. The memorial was unveiled on November 12, 2004 at Beith, the birth place of Faulds. The plaque is depicted here.

The Beith Commemorative Society also released a number of souvenirs in the memory of Faulds, one of which is shown here.

A souvenir in the memory of Dr. Henry Faulds

The fingerprint Society, U.K. also joined hands to give recognition to Faulds. It erected a plaque atop Faulds ancestral home in Beith .

A memento at Faulds ancestral home in Beith

Thanks to the efforts of the Beith Commemorative Society, Dr. Henry Faulds' role as a fingerprint pioneer is now being appreciated and acknowledged.

Epilogue

A PERSON WHO traverses through the story of fingerprinting in India can, in all likelihood, sit back in gratification. India was the first country to realize that each person can be individualized by means of fingerprints. It is, therefore, not surprising that the oldest official documents bearing fingerprints/hand prints can be found in India. It was here that the world's first fingerprint bureau was established. It was here that the formula for classifying fingerprints was invented – and it is a matter of pride for every Indian that more than one hundred years later this classification system is still being used all over the world. It was here that the telegraphic code for and single digit classification of fingerprints were first developed and put into practice.

With the coming of information technology, the fingerprint record-keeping became automated, yet, as compared to other developing nations, India readily adopted the new system. The

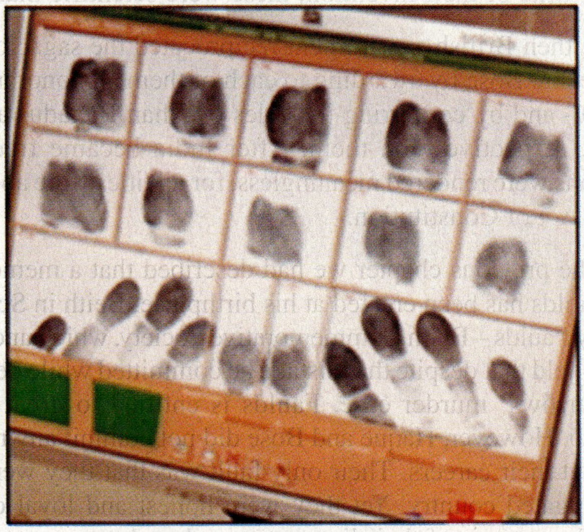

Automated fingerprint identification system

matching of fingerprints, which was earlier done manually, is now carried out with the aid of software, by a technology called *Automated Fingerprint Identification System.*

The Central Fingerprint Bureau at New Delhi has developed a modified version of automated fingerprint identification system, suited to Indian requirements. The system uses image processing and pattern recognition techniques to capture, encode, store and match fingerprints. It also carries out the matching of chance fingerprints.

In spite of all this progress, Indians do feel incensed at lack of recognition accorded to Azizul Haque and Hem Chandra Bose despite their immense contribution to the science of fingerprints. It is now quite clear that Sir Edward Richard Henry actually hoodwinked the Indian officers to falsely claim that he invented the fingerprint classification system. The so called *Henry's System of Fingerprint Classification* was actually worked out jointly by Haque and Bose, while the latter also invented the telegraphic code system for fingerprints, as well as devised the single digit fingerprint classification system. No doubt, the information technology has rendered the telegraphic code and single digit classification obsolete, yet at the time of their invention, these were scientific marvels.

The then British government reciprocated the sagaciousness of Haque and Bose by awarding to each of them an honorarium of Rs. 5000/- and by conferring the titles of Khan Bahadur and Rai Bahadur, respectively on them. After India became free these decorations were rendered meaningless, for all titles were abolished under an Act of Constitution.

In the previous chapter we had described that a memorial to Henry Faulds has been erected at his birthplace, Beith in Scotland. Dr. Henry Faulds – Beith Commemorative Society, which undertook this task, held that despite the mistake he committed while deposing in the Farrows' murder case, Faulds is entitled to great credit. Rightly so. However, Haque and Bose did not commit any mistake throughout their careers. Their only fault was that they were born in a subjugated country. Yet they were honest and loyal officers who, in the autumn of their lives, were reduced to poverty.

Like Dr. Henry Faulds, the role of Azizul Haque and Hem Chandra Bose as pioneers of fingerprint science was never fully acknowledged during their lifetimes. However, in 1997, during the centenary celebrations of the Bengal Fingerprint Bureau, the Department of Post & Telegraph, Government of India issued a special cover portraying Henry, Haque and Bose.

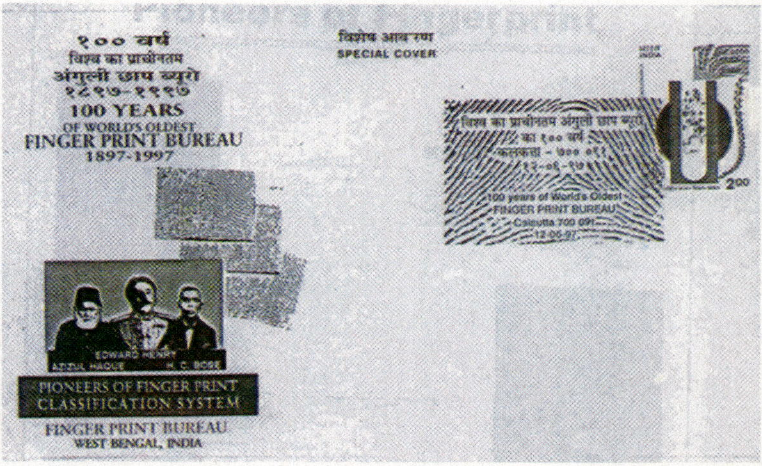

Special cover issued by postal department on the hundredth anniversary of Bengal Fingerprint Bureau

With effect from 2009, the Fingerprint Society, U.K. instituted annual awards in the names of Azizul Haque and Hem Chandra Bose. These are given to meritorious researchers who make a mark in the area of fingerprinting.

The logo of the Fingerprint Society, U.K.

Nevertheless, the true award for a scientist, who has served a global cause, is neither monetary benefit in form of honorarium, nor emblazonment by way of memorabilia, but tagging of his name with his invention. Now that the colonial clouds have dispersed, we suggest that the method of cataloguing criminal record be renamed as *Henry-Haque-Bose System of Fingerprint Classification*.

Additional Readings

Books

1. *E.R. Henry, The Classification and uses of Fingerprints, H.M.S.O., London, 1900.*
2. *W.J. Herschel, The Origin of Finger-Printing, Oxford University Press, London, 1916.*
3. *H.C. Bose, Hints on Finger-Prints with a Telegraphic Code for Finger Impressions, Thacker Spink and Company, Calcutta and Simla, 1916.*
4. *H.C. Bose, Finger Print Companion, Gaudiya Printing Works, Calcutta, 1927.*
5. *F. Galton, Finger Prints, Da Capo Press, New York, 1965.*
6. *S.K. Chatterjee, Finger, Palm and Sole Prints, Kosa Publishers, Calcutta, 1967.*
7. *G. Lambourne, The Fingerprint Story, Harrap, London, 1984.*
8. *J. Berry in Advances in Fingerprint Technology, H.C. Lee & R.E. Gaensslen (Editors), Elsevier, New York, 1991.*

Journals

1. *A.M. Knowles, Aspects of physicochemical methods for the detection of latent fingerprints, Journal of Physics E: Scientific Instrumentation,* ***11*** *(1978) 713-721.*
2. *K.S. Puri, The use of finger and palm prints in ancient India (2), Fingerprint Whorld, July 1980, 21-22.*
3. *B. Wilshire, Advances in fingerprint detection, Endeavour,* ***20****(1) (1996) 12-15.*
4. *G.S. Sodhi and J. Kaur, A tale of two fingerprint experts, Indian Journal of History of Science,* ***36*** *(2001) 151-159.*
5. *G.S. Sodhi and J. Kaur, Sharp eyes saw through early efforts to fake prints, Nature (London),* ***420*** *(2002) 15-16.*

6. *G.S. Sodhi and J. Kaur, The forgotten Indian pioneers of fingerprint science, Current Science, **88** (2005) 185-191.*

Conference Proceedings

1. *P.K. Chattopadhyay, Development of Dactyloscopy in India, Seventh Annual International Meeting of Forensic Sciences, September 8-12, 1975, Zurich, Switzerland.*
2. *G.S. Sodhi and J. Kaur, Indian contribution to the science of fingerprinting, Eighty Eighth Annual International Conference of the International Association for Identification, July 6-11, 2003, Ottawa, Canada.*

Archive Records

1. *Home Department Proceedings No. 124-133(A), Public Branch, May 1896.*
2. *Home Department Proceedings No. 10-16(A), Police Branch, June 1899.*
3. *Home Department Proceedings No. 168-169(A), Public Branch, February 1900.*
4. *Home Department Proceedings No. 141-142(B), Police Branch, October 1917.*
5. *Home Department Proceedings No. 96(B), Police Branch, June 1918.*
6. *Home Department Proceedings No. 202-206(A), Police Branch, August 1919.*
7. *Home Department Proceedings No. F. 112 / 25, Police Branch, 1925.*
8. *Home Department Proceedings No. F. 14 / 29, Police Branch, 1929.*

Biographies

1. *Badshah Nama (the biography of Shah Jahan).*
2. *Tuzuk-i-Jahangiri (the biography of Jahangir).*